GOOD HOUSEKEEPING

QUICK AND EASY
28-Day
Mediterranean Diet

FASTER, SIMPLER RECIPES YOU'LL LOVE FOR LIFE!

GOOD HOUSEKEEPING

QUICK AND EASY
28-Day
Mediterranean Diet

FASTER, SIMPLER RECIPES YOU'LL LOVE FOR LIFE!

Kate Merker
Chief Food Director, Good Housekeeping

Stefani Sassos, MS, RDN, CDN
Registered Dietitian & Nutrition Director, Good Housekeeping Institute

INTRODUCTION

THERE'S NO SECRET as to why the Mediterranean diet has become popular worldwide. Not only does the beloved eating plan, inspired by healthy communities in nations like Greece, Spain, France and Italy, include nutritious, wholesome foods, but it also caters to those who love vibrant recipes and inventive meals. In fact, the Mediterranean diet isn't really a classic diet at all, but more of a healthy eating lifestyle that celebrates some of nature's best foods.

In our *28-Day Mediterranean Diet*, we gave you the tools to master a Mediterranean diet and prep your kitchen for success. We saw just how much the lifestyle worked for you and how sustainable the Mediterranean way of eating felt. In this book, we build on those principles and offer even faster and simpler solutions to following a Mediterranean diet with ease.

This easy-to-follow plan gives you step-by-step guidance for incorporating Mediterranean cuisine and ways of eating into your busy schedule. We talk about how to plan for success when it comes to meal prepping, as well as unique uses for leftovers and easy on-the-go snacking solutions.

But this plan goes beyond food. We'll talk about ways to stay active, get outside and cherish the eating experience with friends and family to help you truly embrace vibrant Mediterranean living wherever you may be. While this plan is meant to serve as a guide that gives you all the tools for success, don't let perfect be the enemy of good. Even if you don't follow the plan flawlessly, you'll still reap immense benefits from whipping up some of the deliciously inventive recipes and incorporating some of the lifestyle tips into everyday living. Cheers to your health journey and embracing the Mediterranean way of life!

Stefani Sassos, MS, RDN, CDN
Registered Dietitian and Nutrition Director,
Good Housekeeping Institute

Kate Merker
Chief Food Director, Good Housekeeping

CONTENTS

RECIPES

THE QUICK & EASY MEDITERRANEAN DIET

What is the Mediterranean Diet?

MANY DIETS ARE burdensome and involve meticulous tracking of macronutrients and timing of your meals. Since the Mediterranean diet is more of a lifestyle and way of eating as opposed to a restrictive weight-loss plan, it makes maintaining healthy eating habits more sustainable in the long run. The approach emphasizes fresh produce, naturally nourishing your body with a plethora of antioxidants, vitamins and minerals. You'll find that those following the Mediterranean diet enjoy plenty of fatty fish (especially salmon, which is considered a staple) alongside whole-grain sides like farro, lots of crisp vegetables and an abundance of supercharged legumes, nuts and seeds. But what you eat on a Mediterranean diet is just as important as how you eat. Shared meals with family and friends is an important cornerstone of the lifestyle. Whether that involves cooking together or sitting together to socialize over your meals, the community and connection aspect of mealtime is part of what makes this approach so special and successful.

Inspired by the eating habits of those in Greece, Spain, Italy and France, among others

Rich in produce, whole grains, lean protein, fatty fish and heart-healthy unsaturated fats

Not based in counting calories or macronutrients, but in selecting wholesome foods

Nothing is completely off-limits (yes, red wine is included, in moderation!)

MEDITERRANEAN DIET BENEFITS

FOLLOW THIS PRODUCE-PACKED WAY OF EATING and you'll start reaping all sorts of benefits. Studies have shown that the Mediterranean diet may:

ASSIST WITH WEIGHT LOSS

You'll be eating more whole foods and fewer ultra-processed ones. Many of the foods on a Mediterranean diet are fiber-rich, which can help keep you full and satisfied. Plus, every delicious dish will provide plenty of vitamins and minerals to help keep you energized.

LOWER HEART DISEASE RISK

Research has shown that the Mediterranean diet may provide heart-healthy benefits. Women who followed the diet had 25% less risk of developing heart disease over the course of 12 years, according to a 2018 study in *JAMA Network Open*. The diet's focus on heart-healthy unsaturated fats, like olive oil instead of butter, is a big contributor to these benefits.

FIGHT INFLAMMATION

Antioxidant-rich foods, like dark leafy greens, avocados and berries, are a staple of the Mediterranean diet. Such foods can combat inflammation and even serve as bodyguards, protecting skin cells from damage. The World Health Organization even recommends the diet to decrease risk of dementia, which has been linked to diets high in inflammatory foods.

IMPROVE GUT HEALTH

People who followed the Mediterranean diet in a 2019 study from the University Medical Center Groningen had a higher amount of "friendly" bacteria in their guts. Since all food is ultimately broken down in the gut, a healthy digestive system is crucial for breaking down and delivering nutrients from these foods throughout the body.

BACK IN 2013, a team of doctors at the University of Barcelona studied more than 7,000 participants who drastically improved their heart health after adopting the Mediterranean diet. The scientific evidence of the diet's effectiveness has piled up since then; a study published in the medical journal *The BMJ* found that elderly individuals may vastly improve brain function and their own longevity by adopting the Mediterranean diet. What's more, research supports that this dietary routine can fight inflammation as we age, stopping the production of chemicals in the body that are known to contribute to cognitive decline and even preventing several major chronic diseases, including diabetes. It's no wonder that Ikaria and Sardinia, islands in Greece and Italy respectively, have both been designated as two of the world's five Blue Zones, or regions where people live the longest.

Not only does the research support its benefits, but many who follow the Mediterranean diet will find that it is different from other weight-loss methods. It's actually less of a diet and more of a lifestyle. Many traditional diets are limited and extreme, which makes them doable for just the short term. A typical restrictive diet may be easy to stick with for a couple of days or weeks, but once the diet is completed it is tempting to revert to old habits and gain all the weight back, especially if you felt forced to give up your favorite foods. Our health and nutrition experts stress that a lifestyle approach to healthy living doesn't have an end date. It's all about building a plan that is flexible, balanced and sustainable for you and your daily needs. The Mediterranean eating plan we've created here includes benefits beyond the number on the scale and will leave you feeling energized, satisfied and excited about your next meal. The whole goal is to keep up with this lifestyle long past the 28 days and have it feel natural and approachable. You'll keep reaping its benefits—from weight loss to improved energy—for as long as you stick with it.

How to Make This Diet Quicker and Easier

You don't need hours upon hours to make delicious and nourishing Mediterranean diet dishes. With the handy hints and shortcuts outlined here, you can spend less time in the kitchen and more time savoring every bite. Here are our favorite time- and effort-saving tips.

FIND YOUR FAVORITE BASE INGREDIENTS

The key to mastering any diet is planning ahead. Whether that involves meal prep, menu planning or just arming your kitchen with staples for success, any work you do ahead of mealtime will make starting (and sticking) to a diet that much easier.

People who live in the Mediterranean regions of the world take time and care when it comes to food shopping, specially selecting each and every item with a focus on freshness. Favorite foods get even more attention, and may come from specialty stores and markets. You may find yourself gravitating toward certain dishes on this plan, so keep a running list of your favorite or most frequently eaten foods as the weeks progress. Select a handful of base ingredients you love and you'll quickly memorize how to prepare them, saving yourself time and effort on busy nights. Plus, when you incorporate favorite ingredients into your weekly menu, you'll look forward to every meal, making it easier to stick to the diet.

Once you have identified those must-have favorite foods, or even foods that you find yourself eating frequently during the week, look for opportunities to batch cook. Cooking every night can be a barrier for many, and when you're short on time it's easy to turn to processed packaged goods or your favorite takeout spot. But batch cooking may just be your solution to sticking to the plan. Grains, firm veggies and certain proteins can be bulk-prepped at the beginning of the week and then added to lunches, dinners and more. Soups, stews and chilis are great make-ahead meals that can be very nutrient-dense and stored in the fridge or freezer for a convenient solution any night. We'll show you exactly how to batch cook some of our favorite ingredients starting on page 34.

Save yourself the time and hassle of making a new dish for every meal by storing leftovers to maintain optimum freshness. Most leftovers can be refrigerated in airtight containers for two to five days, depending on what they are. But there are a few things you can do to make them last longer and taste better the second time around.

Store Separately: Meats and vegetables not only reheat at different rates, but you also may want to use them for different meals in the upcoming days. Storing them separately helps maintain optimal freshness and gives you additional meal-planning flexibility.

Keep It Whole: If you cook steak, pork or chicken and the recipe calls for slicing it, but you know you are not going to eat it all, it is better to keep it whole. That way, it is less likely to dry out, especially if you plan on reheating it.

Hold the Dressing: Instead of tossing or topping with vinaigrettes, tender herbs and greens or crunchy nuts, leave them out and store separately. Drizzle, fold in, sprinkle and add just before serving.

The freezer is your friend when it comes to meal planning! Making a big-batch meal and then storing part of it in the freezer is a great way to set yourself up for easy meals on nights when you're pressed for time. These tips will help keep your freezer well organized.

Clear a Shelf: Your freezer probably also holds other food you use on a regular basis (veggie burgers, frozen fruit for smoothies, etc.). Having one shelf that's dedicated to made-ahead meals will make it easy to store and find things.

Pack Up Your Food: First, let cooked food cool (putting hot food in the freezer is a no-no). Then select your containers. You can use plastic or glass containers (as long as they have airtight lids) or even plastic zip-top freezer bags. Quart-size mason jars are great for soups and stews. It's helpful to divide your food into appropriate portion sizes so you'll only have to defrost what you need. Individual pieces of food (chicken breasts, hamburger patties, slices of pizza, etc.) can be wrapped tightly in plastic wrap and then in aluminum foil.

Label Your Containers: With a Sharpie, write the name of the dish and the date on a piece of mask-

ing tape, then affix the tape to your container before you put it in the freezer.

Last In, First Out: When you put a container of food in the freezer, place it at the back and move older food toward the front. Stack containers to maximize space, making sure you place them so you can see the labels and easily find what you're looking for.

Defrost Safely: The safest way to defrost food (both raw meat or other ingredients, and cooked dishes) is to move it from the freezer to the refrigerator. Small containers can thaw in a few hours, while larger portions may take up to 24 hours or more. When defrosting anything that might leak or drip (like packages of raw meat), place it on a plate or tray before moving to the refrigerator. Once your food is defrosted, use it within a few days. While the overnight thaw is the best and safest way to defrost frozen food, there are other methods if you are pressed for time. Your microwave probably has a defrost setting—check your owner's manual for specifics. If it doesn't, microwave your food in short bursts on low until it thaws. You can also use the cold-water method to thaw smaller cuts of meat like chicken breasts or steaks. Place the meat in a zip-top plastic bag and squeeze out as much air as you can. Submerge the bag in a large bowl of cold water. Change the water every 30 minutes. Smaller cuts (about 1 pound) will thaw in an hour or less, while larger cuts that are 3 to 4 pounds can take 2 to 3 hours. If it's raw meat, cook it immediately (and thoroughly) after it thaws. Never try to defrost meat in hot water at room temp. The FDA says this isn't safe. Once you've thawed raw meat, proceed with your recipe as written. If you're thawing an already-cooked dish, reheat it in the microwave, the oven or on the stovetop.

Use Five-Second Flavor Boosters

There are few faster ways to amp up a meal than with a dash of herbs and spices, and Mediterranean cuisine is filled with these rich flavor makers. A true Mediterranean kitchen is stocked with high-quality spices and herbs, and many include a garden as well to incorporate fresh herbs and produce throughout the week. Regardless of whether your spices and herbs come from the store or are grown at home, they offer tremendous health benefits and provide a fantastic way to add maximum flavor without the need for extra salt. Try these Mediterranean go-tos next time you need to level up a dish in a jiffy:

BASIL

One of the most popular herbs in the world, basil is packed with vibrant flavor and used in a variety of Mediterranean dishes, from vegetables and fish entrées to pesto sauce. Since it grows quickly, it is a great addition to a home garden. Any excess can be dried or even stored in ice cube trays with olive oil then put in the freezer; pop one out and add to a hot skillet for upgraded flavor in any dish.

MINT

This aromatic herb is used throughout the Mediterranean in everything from salads to side dishes and sauces. Mint tea is a staple in the region, and you'll find mint added to grain pilafs and lamb dishes too. Mint plants are also relatively easy to grow.

OREGANO

This fragrant herb is a hallmark of Mediterranean cooking, especially common in Italian, Greek and Turkish cuisines. Fresh oregano has a very strong flavor and can sometimes overpower dishes, so taking advantage of this herb in its dry form can add incredible depth and aroma to everything from tomato-based sauces to vinaigrettes and marinades.

PARSLEY

Colorful and versatile, parsley originated in the Mediterranean and comes in a few different varieties, including flat leaf and curly leaf. But this nutritious herb doesn't have to just be limited to garnishing; it can add brightness to tabbouleh, complement roasted vegetables and even be transformed into a pesto sauce.

SUMAC

This unique spice comes from dried berries of the sumac bush. Typically sold in powder form, sumac has a beautiful red color and a tart, almost lemony flavor. Sumac can help brighten up any flavor profile and works great in meat marinades and on kebabs. Adding some to hummus, whether homemade or store bought, can provide a complementary depth of flavor.

LONG-LASTING MEDITERRANEAN PANTRY INGREDIENTS

You'll reduce trips to the grocery store and will always be prepared to whip up something delicious with these shelf-stable items.

HERBS & SPICES

- ☐ Allspice
- ☐ Basil
- ☐ Bay Leaves
- ☐ Cinnamon
- ☐ Cloves
- ☐ Coriander
- ☐ Crushed Red Pepper Flakes
- ☐ Cumin
- ☐ Dill Weed
- ☐ Garlic Powder
- ☐ Mint
- ☐ Nutmeg
- ☐ Onion Powder
- ☐ Oregano
- ☐ Parsley
- ☐ Rosemary
- ☐ Sage
- ☐ Smoked Paprika
- ☐ Sumac
- ☐ Thyme
- ☐ Turmeric
- ☐ Za'atar

OILS & VINEGARS

- ☐ Apple Cider Vinegar
- ☐ Balsamic Vinegar
- ☐ Extra Virgin Olive Oil
- ☐ Red Wine Vinegar

LEGUMES, NUTS & GRAINS

- ☐ Almonds
- ☐ Barley
- ☐ Buckwheat
- ☐ Bulgur Wheat
- ☐ Cannellini Beans
- ☐ Chickpeas
- ☐ Couscous
- ☐ Farro
- ☐ Fava Beans
- ☐ Kidney Beans
- ☐ Lentils (Red, Yellow and Green)
- ☐ Navy Beans
- ☐ Oats
- ☐ Orzo
- ☐ Pine Nuts
- ☐ Pistachios
- ☐ Quinoa
- ☐ Walnuts
- ☐ Yellow Split Peas

OTHER ESSENTIALS

- ☐ Sesame Seeds
- ☐ Tahini
- ☐ Canned Tomatoes
- ☐ Dry Red & White Wine

Star Ingredients

A Mediterranean kitchen is packed with fresh produce, lean proteins, seafood and healthy fats. These must-have staples make Mediterranean eating easy and are everyday essentials.

BEANS & LENTILS

Legumes are reliable, affordable and versatile staples in many traditional Mediterranean kitchens. They provide a shelf-stable protein source, as well as a slew of vitamins and minerals. Use them to add a dose of filling fiber or some plant-based protein to practically any meal. When choosing canned varieties, opt for low- or reduced-sodium choices.

EGGS

A regular on most grocery lists for good reason, eggs provide a hefty dose of 7 grams of protein each. Boiled eggs are popular in Mediterranean cuisine and make a great snack.

GREEK YOGURT

This popular protein-rich food is incredibly versatile. It makes for a filling snack, a healthy substitute for sour cream and a creamy addition to salad dressings and more. Look for plain varieties that are unsweetened and use berries or your fruit of choice to naturally sweeten your yogurt parfait.

ANCIENT GRAINS

Not only do grains like farro, quinoa, barley, oats and more have great texture and rich flavor, but they are also loaded with nutrients and are celebrated in the Mediterranean diet. Whip up a batch for the week to add to practically any meal.

EXTRA VIRGIN OLIVE OIL

This is the primary oil used in the Mediterranean diet. Traditional uses of olive oil in these regions include everything from salad dressings and roasted vegetables to seafood marinades and dips like hummus. Look for high-quality olive oils that ideally come from a single origin, like Greece, Italy or Spain. When cooking at higher temps, opt for avocado oil, because it has an even higher smoke point.

NUTS & SEEDS

A common daily snack in the Mediterranean, nuts and seeds are packed with protein, healthy fat, vitamins, minerals, fiber and more. They give a burst of sustained energy too, making them the ultimate fuel.

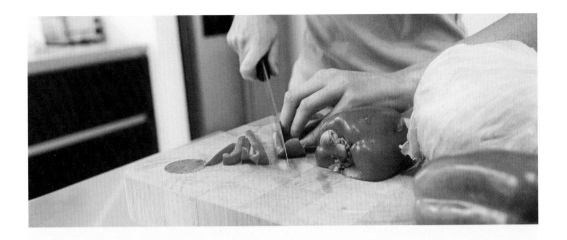

COOK-FASTER TIPS

Borrow from the experts! These pro techniques maximize flavor and results — without adding extra minutes.

CUT SMALL

Slice or dice food into thin or little pieces for quicker cooking: Think thin slices of chicken breast or bell pepper vs. whole or large pieces.

MULTITASK

Start cooking components that take longer earlier. For example, boil the water for pasta right away and get everything else ready in the meantime.

SPREAD IT OUT

When crowded, ingredients steam more than brown. Space food out when you can for the quickest and most flavorful results, or using two pans if necessary.

COVER FOOD

Lids help trap heat and steam. Use them while bringing water or soup to a boil, grilling outdoors or gently reheating foods in a skillet or the microwave.

LEAFY GREENS

A true Mediterranean diet relies heavily on vegetables, and an important component of that group is leafy greens. Every week, keep a bunch on hand, whether it's spinach, kale and arugula or a mixed greens medley. Enjoy them in salad or incorporate them into sautéed dishes, omelets and more.

AVOCADO

Avocados are rich in mono- and polyunsaturated fats, the healthy kinds of fats that are abundant in the Mediterranean diet and actually reduce your risk of heart disease and stroke. If you have any leftover avocado, slice and freeze the rest to add to smoothies and more.

HOW THE PLAN WORKS

Following a diet for 28 days can be easy—with a little bit of strategic planning. We've already done it all for you with a mix of meal prep, batch cooking and some very creative reimaginations of leftovers. Here's a look at how we made following the Mediterranean diet quicker and easier than ever.

5 Ways This Plan Saves You Time and Energy

This plan features strategies that will have you spending less time in the kitchen for the next 28 days. You will:

MEAL PREP BEFORE YOUR WEEK GETS BUSY

For many people, time is short once Monday rolls around. You don't have an hour to spend in front of the stove, so we won't ask you to. Instead, we built this plan so you can partially or fully prepare many of your meals (or elements of each meal) before your week begins. These recipes—found in Chapter 3—are identified by a icon and include "hero" ingredients: foods like hearty grains, versatile proteins, make-ahead breakfasts and even some freezer-friendly soups. Your "hero" ingredients will show up in a few recipes throughout the week, so you get the most

out of each. And if Sunday isn't your least busy day, you can start the meal plan by doing the prep on whatever day works best for you. Just make sure that you start Day 1 of the meal plan the following day to ensure you eat the prepped dishes while they're freshest!

KEEP WEEKDAY COOKING SHORT

By Wednesday night, the temptation for takeout can be strong, which is why we've scheduled your quickest, easiest recipes for Monday through Friday. You'll never spend more than 30 minutes on a weekday meal and some take as little as 5 minutes! And your weeknight efforts will go fur-

ther on this plan since we've built exciting ways to serve up leftovers (yes, it's possible!) into the menu as well.

SWITCH IT UP!

Cravings are often one of the biggest reasons people ditch their diet. Eating leftovers every day can limit the variety of flavors in your diet and leave you desperate for a bite of something different. However, cooking something new each meal is time-consuming, not to mention tiring! The solution? Reinvent your leftovers. Each week you'll find creative and simple ways to make last night's dinner feel fresh. For example, you'll make Roasted White Fish with Cumin Roasted Tomatoes and Chickpeas for Day 2 dinner. On Day 3, you'll transform the leftover tomatoes and chickpeas into a grain bowl with chicken—which uses chicken and farro you prepped on Sunday, so all you'll have to do is cook your grain and do a little assembly and you're done. What's easier than that?

KEEP IT SIMPLE (AND DELICIOUS)

No-stress dishes, like oatmeal, salads and wraps, are staples of any diet, but they don't have to be boring. We've added exciting twists to these quick and reliable standbys without adding a ton of effort. For many, it'll be as simple as sprinkling on an already prepared ingredient or adding a veggie topping. The new flavor combinations you'll create will make all the difference when it comes to staying motivated on the plan.

MAKE JUST WHAT YOU NEED

We perfectly portioned this meal plan to serve one. That means you'll save money and reduce waste since you're making only what you'll eat. If you'd like to make enough food to serve two or four, simply double or quadruple the weekly grocery lists and ingredient quantities for each recipe.

SPEED-CLEANING SECRETS

Quick meals are great. Quick cleanup is even better! Brush up on these time-saving tips approved by our GH Cleaning Lab.

STAY ORGANIZED

Clear, labeled containers make it easier to find what you need, and keeping similar things (such as all bowls) in the same place makes prepping more efficient.

CORRAL TRASH

To limit garbage can trips, keep a small bowl next to your cutting board for scraps.

CLEAN AS YOU GO

Trained cooks are taught to wash pots, pans and utensils as soon as they're done using them, but you can start by emptying your dishwasher before you cook. Then put dirty items directly into it instead of cluttering the sink.

CONTAIN MESSES

Measure and level ingredients like flour, sugar and salt over the sink or a sheet of waxed paper so you can rinse away or contain spills and keep counters clean.

LIMIT TASTING UTENSILS

Instead of employing a vast number of utensils to avoid double-dipping, use a serving utensil to move a small amount onto your own dish.

Fast FAQs

You might have some questions as you make your way through the 28-day meal plan. Here, find the answers to the most frequently asked ones so you'll never miss a beat.

DOES IT MATTER WHAT BRAND OF FOOD I BUY?

Feel free to buy what you prefer. Just remember:
- The fewer ingredients on the label, the better.
- Always check to see if the first ingredient is a whole real food, as the ingredients are listed by weight.
- Keep an eye out for added sugar. For packaged goods like Greek yogurt or granola, aim to keep sugar at a minimum—no more than 8 grams added sugar per serving.

CAN I DRINK ALCOHOL ON THIS PLAN?

A Mediterranean diet customarily allows red wine in moderation—one drink (equivalent to about 5 oz of wine) a day or less for women and two drinks a day or less for men. Speak with your doctor before incorporating this into the plan, though. And avoid it altogether in certain situations, such as if you are on a medication that interacts with alcohol or you are recovering from an alcohol use disorder.

CAN I MAKE INGREDIENT SWAPS BASED ON TASTE OR DIETARY RESTRICTION?

Absolutely! Most grains and regular breads can easily be swapped out for gluten-free options, but try to stick with varieties that are minimally processed, if possible. For vegetarians, feel free to experiment with vegan protein sources like tofu and tempeh. Beans and lentils are great too—in fact, they are cornerstones of this diet. There's also a variety of dairy-free options made from cashews and chickpeas that would work well to substitute for cheese in most recipes.

WILL THIS PLAN HELP ME LOSE WEIGHT?

You'll find that each day is packed with nutrient-dense foods that can help support a healthy weight. We've created each day to hit around 1,500 calories as a base so you have room to add in your favorite foods (and beverages like a glass of wine or two throughout the week). The plan is designed to be built upon by doubling, tripling or even quadrupling your servings of veggies at any opportunity and adding more fruits at snack time too. The combo of fiber from produce and lean protein makes this an adaptable strategy that'll help you successfully manage your weight and promote healthy choices. If you are trying to lose weight, our experts suggest keeping any extras to the existing plan to a total of 300 to 500 calories per day.

WHAT IF I MISS A DAY?

No worries! Get right back on track with the plan and resume it the next day—no detoxing or extreme restrictions needed. Just recommit as best you can.

HOW CAN I INCORPORATE DINING OUT INTO THIS LIFESTYLE AFTER THE 28 DAYS?

Two easy ways to keep this lifestyle:

Prioritize plant-based. Aim to have a salad, a veggie-based soup or produce-powered side dish with every meal.

Rely on keywords. Look for terms on the menu that indicate healthier prep methods like:

- Baked
- Steamed
- Roasted
- Broiled
- Grilled
- Poached
- Seared
- Lightly sautéed

SHOULD I EAT MY MEALS AT A CERTAIN TIME?

A good rule of thumb is to eat something every three to four hours during the day. Going too long without food may cause you to feel ravenous and reach for a quick fix. But the best times to eat are dictated by your body. Practice listening to your body and becoming familiar with your hunger cues. By slowing down and learning to eat mindfully, you can not only make nutritious food choices but also foster a healthy relationship with food and your body. Here are some tips for eating mindfully, an important pillar of the Mediterranean lifestyle:

EXAMINE YOUR HUNGER AND APPETITE

Hunger is your physiological need for food, whereas appetite is your desire for food. Try to examine how your body is feeling at the beginning of a meal; are you actually eating out of boredom or anxiety instead of hunger? Conversely, have you let your body go too long without food? Slight hunger is OK, but anything more severe can make it difficult to slow down and eat mindfully. Commit to incorporating balanced meals throughout the day so you have an appetite at mealtimes but aren't ravenous.

START WITH GRATITUDE

Take a minute or two to pause and appreciate the food in front of you. Choose to be present and focus on gratitude for your body, the incredible meal and everything and everyone that went into preparing it. Are you sharing this eating experience with any friends or family? Take a moment to reflect and express your gratitude for them too.

LIMIT DISTRACTIONS

In order to fully immerse yourself in mindful eating, it's important to disconnect from electronics and major distractions. Silence your phone, turn off the TV, and sit down at the kitchen table so you are fully present in the meal.

UTILIZE YOUR SENSES

Pay attention to the different flavor profiles in your meal and the aroma of the food. Ask yourself questions like these: How does the food sound when you chew it? Does it feel crunchy or smooth when you take a bite? What flavor notes do you detect? Do any of these tastes or textures change as you continue eating the meal? Paying full attention to your food enhances the mindful eating experience.

SLOW DOWN

Take time to chew your food, savor the flavor and appreciate each bite. If you find that you're still eating quickly, try to set your fork down after every few bites. It takes about 20 minutes for your stomach to signal to your brain that it's full. Give yourself time to digest and get in tune with satiety, the feeling of fullness and satisfaction that you get from eating.

Elements of the Meal Plan

Our food and nutrition experts designed this plan to be effortless, simple and practical. We include tons of resources and tools to help you navigate the common obstacles that come with sticking with any healthy eating plan. Here's exactly what you will find and how best to use it:

WEEK AT-A-GLANCE

This brief overview gives you an idea of what to expect for your meals at the beginning of each week and how any left-overs will be repurposed. We give important tips on planning ahead, so it's a good idea to take a look at this in advance to be prepared.

WEEKLY SHOPPING LIST

Nothing derails a diet faster than a missing ingredient. Our comprehensive shopping lists ensure you have everything you need on hand and in the correct quantity for every meal and snack for the week. Snap a photo and reference it on your grocery run.

GET-AHEAD GAME PLAN

To help you have the easiest week(s) ever, we'll pinpoint which dishes and ingredients you should meal prep at the start of the week.

BONUS TRACKER PAGES

The Mediterranean diet is a lifestyle that doesn't need to end after 28 days. We included extra pages at the end of the meal plan to encourage you to track the above details and create your own daily menus.

DAILY MENUS

Each day of the plan has exactly what you will be eating that day, plus a wellness tracker to log your daily movement, hydration and other elements.

Wellness Tracker Basics

Want to get even more out of the plan? Take note of your overall wellness by logging your progress in these 5 key areas using the wellness tracker pages.

WATER: Staying hydrated is important to keeping your body happy and healthy. It's easy to confuse your need for water with hunger, so knowing how much you need each day is essential. For the average person, about eight cups a day is a reasonable goal. For a more accurate estimate, try to drink a half ounce of water for each pound you weigh. So if you weigh 160 lbs, you'll need 80 oz of water, or 10 cups. While it's good to reach your hydration goals primarily with water, you can also drink sparkling water, unsweetened coffee and tea or fruit-infused water. It also helps to consume high-water-content foods like cucumber, tomatoes, watermelon, asparagus, grapes and celery. They'll hydrate you and keep you full due to their higher fiber content.

MOVEMENT: Regular exercise is vital to any health regimen, but physical activity isn't limited to what happens in the gym. Day-to-day activities and chores such as a couple of hours walking the mall while shopping or spending 30 minutes raking leaves still count and tracking these activities may even motivate you to do more.

The American Heart Association recommends 150 minutes of moderate-intensity aerobic activity or 75 minutes of vigorous-intensity aerobic activity, or a combination of both, preferably spread throughout the week. This plan gives you space to note the type of activity you performed, how long you did it for and the intensity at which you did it. For a mood booster, review your log at the end of the week. You may find that you did more than you thought! Remember:

Always consult with your physician or health care practitioner before starting any exercise regimen.

SLEEP: Quality shut-eye is a critical component of your ability to stick with any health plan. When you're tired, you're more likely to cave to cravings, make food decisions you wouldn't otherwise consider, lose focus on your goals, lack the energy to get the quality movement you need for overall wellness or engage in social activities (which have their own weight-loss benefits!). Keep an eye on how sleep impacts your waking life by noting your bedtime and wake-up time each day, as well as if it affected your cravings or ability to stick with the plan.

MOOD: Less-than-perfect days are part of life, so being aware of them is a productive step to not letting them get the best of you. Use the mood tracker to identify your general mood and make a few notes about what might have caused it, how it impacted your plan or ideas for how to handle things next time.

CONNECTION: Meals are a great opportunity to shift the focus from nourishment to connection. With eating as a shared experience, you will likely find that you eat more slowly, especially when holding a conversation. This gives you time to tune into your satiety signals instead of quickly polishing off your plate. Use this space to write down how you connected with others. It can take the form of a shared meal or simply a phone call with a friend.

Before You Begin

Complete this page to get a sense of where you are as you're starting out and to set goals for the next 28 days. Refer back whenever you need a boost—and to see how far you've come!

DATE:

I AM STARTING THIS PLAN BECAUSE:

AT THE END OF THIS PLAN, I WANT TO FEEL:

MY CURRENT WATER INTAKE IS USUALLY:

MY CURRENT MOVEMENT IS USUALLY:

MY CURRENT SLEEP IS USUALLY:

MY CURRENT MOOD IS USUALLY:

MY CURRENT CONNECTION IS USUALLY:

MEAL PREP RECIPES

Your Sunday prep work will consist of three different types of strategies. You'll cook large batches of ingredients that keep well throughout the week, including grains, vegetables and proteins. You'll also get many of your breakfasts ready, so mornings are a breeze. Finally, some weeks you'll whip up a big pot of soup, which you can refrigerate or freeze, then thaw when needed.

Basic Meal Prep

Devote some time to cooking up some proteins, grains and vegetables that you can add to recipes throughout the week. Below, find tried-and-tested cooking times—plus storage tips—so you can maximize your meal-prepping efforts.

GRAINS

How to store cooked grains: First, let grains cool completely, then refrigerate in an airtight container for up to five days. Or store them in the freezer for a month or more. To freeze, transfer enough grain to a reusable bag to create a thin layer; use enough bags until all your grain is bagged, then stack bags in the freezer (the thinner a layer, the faster the defrosting!). To reheat, microwave for a minute or two.

GRAIN	GRAIN TO WATER (CUPS)	STOVETOP INSTRUCTIONS	YIELD (CUPS)
Quinoa, rinsed	1:2	Bring quinoa and water to a boil; cover and simmer on low until water is absorbed and quinoa is tender, about 15 min. Remove from heat and let stand, covered, 5 min.	3
Farro (pearled), rinsed	1½:10	Bring water to a boil. Add farro and cook, stirring occasionally, until firm yet tender, 20 to 30 min. Drain.	3½
Brown rice (short-grain), rinsed	1:1.75	Bring rice and water to a boil; cover and simmer on low until water is absorbed and rice is tender, 40 to 45 min. Remove from heat and let stand, covered, 10 min.	3
Couscous	1½:1½	Bring water to a boil, then stir in couscous. Immediately remove from heat and let stand, covered, 5 min.	4
Bulgur	1:2	Bring water to a boil, then stir in bulgur. Cover and simmer on low until water is absorbed and bulgur is tender, about 15 min. Remove from heat and let stand, covered, 10 min.	3
Barley (pearled), rinsed	1:8	Bring water to a boil. Add barley and cook, like pasta, until firm yet tender, 25 to 30 min. Drain.	2¾

VEGETABLES

Before roasting or air-frying, prep, toss in olive oil, season with salt and pepper and then spread out on a baking sheet or in the air fryer. Toss once or twice while they're in the oven or air-fryer.

VEGETABLE	PREP	ROAST AT 450°F	AIR FRYER
Brussels sprouts	Trimmed and halved (or quartered if large)	15 to 20 min.	375°F 10 to 12 min.
Broccoli + cauliflower	Cut into small florets	16 to 20 min.	380°F 6 to 8 min.
Carrots + parsnips	Peeled, halved lengthwise and cut into 2-in. pieces (halved or quartered again lengthwise if thick)	17 to 20 min.	380°F 12 to 15 min.
Sweet potato + butternut squash	Peeled and cut into 1-in. pieces	22 to 25 min.	400°F 30 min.
Bell peppers	Cut into 1-in. pieces	15 to 20 min.	400°F 10 min.
Mushrooms	Halved or quartered if large	9 to 12 min.	400°F 8 min. (oyster)
Green beans + asparagus	Trimmed then halved or cut into 2 1/2-in. pieces	8 to 12 min.	385°F 5 min.
Onions	Sliced 1/2-in. thick	13 to 16 min.	400°F 10 min.
Grape/cherry tomatoes	Keep whole	10 to 13 min.	400°F 15 to 20 min.

PROTEINS

BONELESS SKINLESS CHICKEN BREAST (5 TO 6 OZ)

Sear: Season with salt and pepper and cook in skillet in olive oil on medium until golden brown and cooked through, 5 to 7 min. per side.
Grill: Rub with olive oil, season with salt and pepper and grill on medium-high until cooked through, 4 to 6 min. per side.

FLANK STEAK

Season with salt and pepper, cook per directions and let rest at least 5 min. before slicing.

Broil: On a baking sheet, broil to desired doneness, 8 min. for medium-rare.
Grill: Grill on medium-high, covered, 4 min. Flip and grill to desired doneness, 3 to 5 min. more for medium-rare.
Air-Fry: Air-fry at 400°F to desired doneness, 8 to 10 min. for medium-rare.

SALMON FILLET (5 TO 6 OZ)

Brush with olive oil, season with salt and pepper and cook per directions until opaque throughout.

Sear: Cook in a nonstick skillet in olive oil on medium until golden brown, 7 min. Flip and cook about 2 min. more.
Broil: Place on foil-lined baking sheet and broil 2 to 3 min. per side.
Roast: Place on foil-lined baking sheet and roast at 450°F, 8 to 10 min.
Air Fry: Air-fry at 400°F, 8 to 10 min.
Grill: Grill on medium-high 3 to 5 min. per side.

SAUCES

CREAMY FETA SAUCE

ACTIVE 5 min.
TOTAL 5 min.
Makes 1 cup

- ½ cup milk
- 4 oz (⅔ cup) feta, crumbled
- 2 Tbsp fresh lemon juice
- 1 tsp lemon zest
- ¼ tsp kosher salt
- ¼ tsp pepper

In mini food processor, puree all ingredients until smooth.

GREEN OLIVE VINAIGRETTE

ACTIVE 5 min.
TOTAL 5 min.
Makes ½ cup

- ½ cup pitted Castelvetrano olives
- ¼ cup olive oil
- 1 Tbsp fresh lemon juice
- ½ tsp Dijon mustard
- 1 clove garlic
- 2 Tbsp chopped flat-leaf parsley
- 1 tsp nutritional yeast

In mini food processor, process olives, olive oil, lemon juice, Dijon and garlic until smooth, 2 min. Transfer to medium bowl then fold in parsley and nutritional yeast.

MOJO-STYLE SAUCE

ACTIVE 10 min.
TOTAL 10 min.
Makes ¾ cup

- 1½ cups cilantro leaves and stems
- ¼ cup fresh orange juice
- ¼ cup olive oil
- 2 Tbsp fresh lime juice
- ½ tsp kosher salt
- ¼ tsp red pepper flakes
- 1 small shallot, chopped
- 1 small garlic clove

In blender, blend all ingredients on high until homogenous but still bright green, 30 sec.

TANGY TAHINI SAUCE

ACTIVE 5 min.
TOTAL 5 min.
Makes ¾ cup

- ½ cup tahini
- 2 Tbsp white wine vinegar
- 1 tsp pure maple syrup
- ½ tsp kosher salt
- ¼ tsp pepper

In medium bowl, whisk together all ingredients with ¼ cup water. If needed, whisk in 1 Tbsp more water at a time until creamy.

MAKE-AHEAD
BREAKFASTS

Herbed Egg Bites

ACTIVE TIME 10 MIN. | TOTAL TIME 30 MIN.

Olive oil, for muffin pan
6   large eggs
¼   cup sour cream
¼   cup milk
¼   tsp kosher salt
¼   tsp pepper
1   cup flat-leaf parsley, chopped
½   cup dill, chopped
¼   cup chopped chives

1. Heat oven to 350°F and oil 12-cup muffin pan.

2. In large measuring cup or bowl, whisk together eggs, sour cream, milk, salt and pepper. Mix in parsley, dill and chives.

3. Divide egg mixture among prepared cups (about ¼ cup each). Bake until just set in center, 12 to 15 min. Let cool 5 min., then remove from pan.

MAKES 12 *About 54 cal, 4 g fat (1.5 g sat), 4 g pro, 82 mg sodium, 1 g carb, 0 g fiber*

MAKE IT AHEAD
Transfer to an airtight container and refrigerate up to 4 days or freeze in muffin tin until firm, then transfer to container or bag, squeezing out excess air and freeze up to 1 month. When ready to eat, microwave on medium until heated through.

Jammy Eggs

ACTIVE TIME 10 MIN. | TOTAL TIME 15 MIN.

2   eggs

1. Bring medium saucepan of water to a boil and fill medium bowl with ice water.

2. Reduce heat so water is at rapid simmer, gently add eggs and simmer 6 min. Immediately transfer eggs to ice water to stop cooking. Drain and refrigerate for up to 5 days. Peel when ready to use.

MAKES 2 *About 70 cal, 5 g fat (1.5 g sat), 6 g pro, 150 mg sodium, 0 g carb, 0 g fiber*

PREP-AHEAD
EGGS MAKE THIS
JAMMY EGG TOAST
(P. 92) AN EASY
ANYTIME
BREAKFAST.

Almond Buckwheat Granola

ACTIVE TIME 30 MIN. | TOTAL TIME 30 MIN.

1   Tbsp olive oil
1   Tbsp pure maple syrup
¼   tsp kosher salt
½   cup buckwheat groats
¼   tsp ground cinnamon
⅓   cup sliced almonds

1. Heat oven to 300°F. Line small rimmed baking sheet with parchment paper. In small bowl, whisk together oil, maple syrup and salt.

2. Heat medium cast-iron skillet on medium-high. Add groats and toast, shaking and tossing often and adjusting heat as needed, until color and aroma deepen and groats are crisp, 1 to 2 min.

3. Transfer to bowl with maple syrup mixture and toss to coat (it will sizzle), then stir in cinnamon and almonds. Spread onto prepared baking sheet and bake, stirring halfway through, until golden brown, 15 to 20 min. Let cool. Store in an airtight container for up to 10 days.

SERVES 4 *About 105 cal, 7 g fat (1 g sat), 2 g pro, 150 mg sodium, 9 g carb, 1.5 g fiber*

Zucchini Bread

ACTIVE TIME 20 MIN. | TOTAL TIME 1 HR. 10 MIN. PLUS COOLING

¾ cup olive oil (or canola oil), plus more for pan

1¾ cups all-purpose flour

1 tsp ground cinnamon

½ tsp baking soda

½ tsp baking powder

½ tsp kosher salt

¼ tsp freshly grated nutmeg

2 large eggs

½ cup packed light brown sugar

¼ cup granulated sugar

1 tsp pure vanilla extract

½ lb small zucchini (about 2)

1 cup walnuts, roughly chopped, divided

1. Heat oven to 350°F. Lightly oil 8½- by 4½-in. loaf pan. Line with parchment paper, leaving overhang on 2 long sides; lightly oil paper.

2. In medium bowl, whisk together flour, cinnamon, baking soda, baking powder, salt and nutmeg.

3. In large bowl, beat eggs. Add sugars and remaining oil, beat until combined, then mix in vanilla. Add dry ingredients, mixing until just incorporated.

4. Grate zucchini on large holes of box grater and fold into batter along with ½ cup walnuts. Transfer to prepared pan and sprinkle with remaining ½ cup walnuts. Bake until wooden pick inserted into center comes out clean, 65 to 75 min. Let cool in pan 15 min., then use overhangs to transfer to wire rack to cool completely.

5. Wrap and refrigerate for up to a week, slicing as needed. Or slice, arrange on a parchment-lined baking sheet and freeze until firm, then wrap each slice and freeze for up to 2 months.

SERVES 16 *About 240 cal, 16 g fat (2 g sat), 4 g pro, 129 mg sodium, 22 g carb, 1 g fiber*

Citrus-Spiced Overnight Oats

½ cup cashew milk,
plus more for serving

½ tsp honey, warmed,
plus more for drizzling
if desired

½ tsp orange zest
plus ¾ cup juice

¼ tsp grated nutmeg

⅛ tsp ground cinnamon
Small pinch kosher salt
Small pinch ground
cardamom

6 Tbsp rolled oats

½ Tbsp chia seeds

1 small orange, peeled
and cut into segments

2 Tbsp walnuts, toasted
and chopped
Pomegranate arils,
for serving

1. In bowl, whisk together cashew milk, honey, orange zest and juice, nutmeg, cinnamon, salt and cardamom. Stir in oats and chia seeds. Cover and refrigerate overnight.

2. To serve, adjust consistency with more cashew milk if desired. Roughly chop half of orange segments and fold into oats along with half of walnuts. Top with remaining whole orange segments, chopped walnuts, additional honey, and pomegranate arils if desired.

SERVES 1 *About 375 cal, 14 g fat (1.5 g sat), 9 g pro, 200 mg sodium, 58 g carb, 8 g fiber*

Buckwheat and Fig Muffins

ACTIVE TIME 25 MIN. | TOTAL TIME 45 MIN.

1	cup buckwheat flour
½	cup oat flour
1	tsp baking powder
½	tsp baking soda
½	tsp kosher salt
1	large egg, beaten
1	cup plain full-fat yogurt
¼	cup milk
3	Tbsp honey
16	fresh figs, 12 finely chopped and 4 thinly sliced

1. Heat oven to 400°F. Lightly coat a 12-cup muffin pan with nonstick cooking spray.

2. In large bowl, whisk flours, baking powder, baking soda and salt. In medium bowl, whisk together egg, yogurt, milk and honey. Fold egg mixture into flour mixture; fold in chopped figs.

3. Divide batter among muffin cups (about ¼ cup each) and top each with 2 to 3 fig slices. Bake until toothpick inserted into centers of muffins comes out clean, 15 to 20 min. Let cool 5 min., then transfer to wire rack to cool completely.

MAKES 12 *About 113 cal, 2 g fat (1 g sat), 3 g pro, 198 mg sodium, 22 g carb, 2 g fiber*

MAKE IT AHEAD
Freeze muffins in muffin tin until firm, then transfer to freezer-safe bag, squeezing out excess air; freeze up to 2 months. When ready to eat, wrap in paper towel and microwave at 50% power until heated through, 1 to 2 min.

Spinach-Artichoke Frittata

ACTIVE TIME 40 MIN. | TOTAL TIME 40 MIN.

10	large eggs
3/4	tsp grated nutmeg
2/3	cup grated Parmesan, divided
	Kosher salt and pepper
2	Tbsp olive oil, divided
1	12-oz pkg. frozen quartered artichoke hearts, thawed and patted dry
4	scallions, thinly sliced
2	cloves garlic, finely chopped
5	oz baby spinach

1. Heat oven to 400°F. In large bowl, whisk together eggs until no streaks remain and whisk in nutmeg, half of cheese and ¼ tsp each salt and pepper.

2. Heat 1½ Tbsp oil in 10-in. cast-iron skillet on medium. Add artichokes, season with ½ tsp salt and cook, turning occasionally, until golden brown, adjusting heat if necessary, 7 to 8 min.; transfer to plate.

3. Add remaining ½ Tbsp oil to skillet along with scallions and cook, stirring, 30 sec.; stir in garlic then add spinach and cover until beginning to wilt, 1 min. Uncover and cook, stirring, until completely wilted, 1 more min.

4. Stir in egg mixture to coat vegetables, then cook until edges begin to set, 2 min. Arrange artichokes on top and sprinkle with remaining cheese. Bake until golden brown and just fully set, 12 min. Let rest 8 to 10 min. and serve.

SERVES 8 *About 180 cal, 11.5 g fat (3.5 g sat), 11 g pro, 440 mg sodium, 7 g carb, 4 g fiber*

MAKE IT AHEAD

Make frittata, let cool, then cut into pieces. Refrigerate in an airtight container for up to 3 days or wrap each piece and freeze for up to 2 months. Rewarm: Frozen frittata can be wrapped in damp paper towel and microwaved at 50% power for 3 min.

Mango Passion Fruit Chia Overnight Shake

ACTIVE TIME 15 MIN. | TOTAL TIME 2½ TO 8 HR.

1 ripe mango, peeled and cut into chunks (about 11 oz total)

⅓ cup frozen passion fruit pieces, thawed (we used Pitaya brand)

½ cup cashew milk, or milk of choice, plus more for serving

½ tsp pure vanilla extract

½ tsp pure maple syrup
Pinch kosher salt

½ Tbsp chia seeds

½ Tbsp finely shredded unsweetened coconut, toasted (see Note)

1. In blender, puree mangos, passion fruit, milk, vanilla, maple syrup and salt until smooth.

2. Place chia seeds in medium bowl and whisk in mango mixture. Refrigerate overnight.

3. Stir coconut into chia-mango mixture, adjusting consistency with more milk if necessary.

SERVES 1 *About 300 cal, 5.5 g fat (2 g sat), 5 g pro, 200 mg sodium, 62 g carb, 7 g fiber*

NOTE
To toast coconut, heat oven or toaster oven to 350°F. Spread 4 Tbsp finely shredded unsweetened coconut on small parchment-lined baking sheet. Bake, tossing halfway through, until golden brown, 3 to 3 1/2 min.

Banana Chocolate Chip Muffins

ACTIVE TIME 15 MIN. | TOTAL TIME 40 MIN.

3   large ripe bananas (1½ cups)
2   large eggs
⅓   cup pure maple syrup
¼   cup coconut oil, melted
2   Tbsp milk
2   tsp pure vanilla extract
2   cups old-fashioned oats
1   tsp baking powder
1   tsp baking soda
¼   tsp kosher salt
½   cup bittersweet chocolate chips, divided
1   cup flaked coconut

1. Heat oven to 350°F. Line a 12-cup muffin pan with paper liners.

2. In blender, place bananas, eggs, maple syrup, coconut oil, milk and vanilla. Top with oats, baking powder, baking soda and salt. Puree until smooth. Add ¼ cup chocolate chips and pulse twice.

3. Divide among muffin cups and top with coconut and remaining chips. Bake until a toothpick inserted into the center comes out clean, 18 to 22 min.

MAKES 12 *About 235 cal, 13 g fat (9 g sat), 4 g pro, 205 mg sodium, 28 g carb, 4 g fiber*

FREEZER-FRIENDLY MAINS

Air Fryer Squash Soup

ACTIVE TIME 20 MIN. | TOTAL TIME 45 MIN.

2½ lbs butternut squash, peeled, cut into 1-in. pieces

2 medium carrots, cut into 1-in. pieces

1 large onion, cut into ½-in.-thick wedges

4 cloves garlic, 2 whole and 2 thinly sliced, divided

1 Fresno chile, seeded

4 sprigs fresh thyme

4 Tbsp olive oil, divided
Kosher salt

2 Tbsp pepitas

¼ tsp smoked paprika
Sour cream and crusty bread, for serving

1. In large bowl, toss squash, carrots, onion, whole garlic cloves, chile, thyme, 2 Tbsp oil and ¾ tsp salt. Transfer to air fryer basket and air-fry at 400°F, shaking basket occasionally, until vegetables are tender, 30 min. Discard thyme sprigs.

2. Meanwhile, in small skillet on medium, cook sliced garlic in remaining 2 Tbsp oil, stirring, until garlic begins to lightly brown around the edges, 2 min. Add pepitas and paprika and a pinch salt and cook 1 min.; transfer to a bowl.

3. Transfer all but ½ cup squash to blender, add 1 cup water and puree, gradually adding 3 more cups water, pureeing until smooth. Reheat if necessary and serve topped with sour cream and spiced pepitas and with crusty bread if desired. Serve topped with remaining squash.

SERVES 4 *About 280 cal, 15.5 g fat (2.5 g sat), 5 g pro, 425 mg sodium, 36 g carb, 7 g fiber*

MAKE IT AHEAD
Refrigerate pureed soup without sour cream and spiced pepitas for up to 5 days or freeze for up to 2 months. Reheat when ready to eat and serve topped with sour cream and a sprinkle of smoked paprika, if desired.

Freezing Soups 101

WAIT IT OUT

Allow soups to cool completely before transferring to (single-serving) freezer-safe airtight containers and storing in the freezer. Be sure to label with the date.

BE CHOOSY

Skip freezing soups with pasta, potatoes or rice as these ingredients can get gummy. Instead, add your starch when reheating.

TAKE TIME TO THAW

When you're ready to reheat, thaw soups in the fridge overnight, then add to a pot over medium heat, stirring occasionally, until warmed through, adding in any starches you left out, 10 minutes.

Tomato, White Bean and Vegetable Soup

ACTIVE TIME 25 MIN. | TOTAL TIME 30 MIN.

2   Tbsp olive oil
1   large onion, chopped
2   medium carrots,
     cut into ¼-in. pieces
1   stalk celery,
     cut into ¼-in. pieces
1   small bulb fennel,
     cut into ¼-in. pieces
     Kosher salt and pepper
2   large cloves garlic,
     finely chopped
6   sprigs fresh thyme
½   cup dry white wine
1   28-oz can whole
     peeled tomatoes
1   Tbsp chicken or vegetable
     base (optional)
4   oz short pasta
2   15-oz cans white beans
     (cannellini, navy, butter
     or a combination), rinsed
     Chopped parsley and
     grated Parmesan,
     for serving

1. Heat oil in large Dutch oven on medium. Add onion and cook, stirring occasionally, 5 min. Add carrots, celery, fennel, ¾ tsp salt and ½ tsp pepper and cook, covered, stirring occasionally, until vegetables are beginning to soften, 6 to 8 min. more. Stir in garlic and thyme and cook 2 min. Add wine and simmer until nearly evaporated, 1 to 2 min.

2. Add tomatoes and their juices, crushing into small pieces as you add to pot. Add 5 cups water and chicken base (if using) and pasta and bring to a boil, stirring often. Simmer, stirring often until barely tender, 4 to 10 min. depending on type of pasta. Stir in beans and cook until heated through, about 2 min. Remove thyme and serve sprinkled with parsley and Parmesan.

SERVES 6 *About 460 cal, 6.5 g fat (1.5 g sat), 20 g pro, 820 mg sodium, 81 g carb, 18 g fiber*

MAKE IT AHEAD
Make soup without pasta and refrigerate for up to 5 days. Add pasta while reheating.

Pepper and Onion Pizza

ACTIVE TIME 10 MIN. | TOTAL TIME 20 MIN.

Flour, for surface

1 lb pizza dough,
at room temperature

Cornmeal,
for baking sheet

½ oz extra-sharp Cheddar,
coarsely grated

1 small onion, thinly sliced

1 small red pepper, sliced

1 small yellow pepper, sliced

1 poblano pepper, halved
and thinly sliced

1 small jalapeño, halved
and thinly sliced

1 Tbsp olive oil

Kosher salt and pepper

1. Heat oven to 500°F (if you can't heat the oven this high without broiling, heat to 475°F).

2. On a lightly floured surface, shape the pizza dough into a 14-in. oval. Place on a cornmeal-dusted or parchment-lined baking sheet. Sprinkle Cheddar over top.

3. In a large bowl, toss onion and peppers with olive oil and ¼ tsp each salt and pepper. Scatter over dough and bake until the crust is golden brown, 10 to 12 min.

SERVES 4 *About 330 cal, 6.5 g fat (1.5 g sat), 12 g pro, 690 mg sodium, 57 g carb, 3 g fiber*

MAKE IT AHEAD

Let any leftover pizza come to room temp. Portion as desired, wrap in foil and freeze in an airtight container or bag for up to 2 months. Cook from frozen directly on oven rack at 400°F until heated through and crisp, 10 to 15 min.

Falafel

ACTIVE TIME 15 MIN. | TOTAL TIME 35 MIN.

2   cloves garlic
4   scallions, white parts only,
    thinly sliced
½   cup baby kale
2   15-oz cans chickpeas,
    drained and rinsed
1   tsp grated lemon zest
2   Tbsp all-purpose flour
1   tsp ground cumin
1   tsp ground coriander
    Kosher salt
1   Tbsp olive oil, plus more
    for baking

1. In food processor, pulse garlic, scallion whites and baby kale until very finely chopped. Add chickpeas, lemon zest, flour, cumin, coriander and ½ tsp salt and pulse to combine (chickpeas should be chopped but coarse). Form mixture into 24 balls, 2 Tbsp each.

2. Heat air fryer to 325°F. Brush insert of basket with oil and add 12 falafel. Air-fry 15 min. Brush falafel with 1 Tbsp oil and increase air fryer temperature to 400°F. Air-fry until deeply golden, 4 more min. Repeat with remaining falafel. Refrigerate falafel for up to 5 days or freeze for up to 1 month.

SERVES 4 *About 230 cal, 7 g fat (1 g sat), 10 g pro, 520 mg sodium, 34 carb, 9 g fiber*

**MAKE
IT AHEAD**
*Arrange falafel on
rimmed baking sheet and
freeze until firm, then transfer to
freezer-safe container and
freeze up to 1 month. Air-fry
from frozen at 375°F until
heated through,
10 to 15 min.*

THIS SALAD
(P. 170) COMES
TOGETHER QUICKLY
WHEN YOU MAKE
THE FALAFEL
IN ADVANCE.

THE
MEAL
PLAN

STOCK YOUR PANTRY

Be sure to always have these essentials on hand throughout the meal plan.

- Aleppo pepper
- All-purpose flour
- Baking powder
- Baking soda
- Dijon mustard
- Dried oregano
- Granulated sugar

- Grated nutmeg
- Ground allspice
- Ground cinnamon
- Honey
- Kosher salt
- Maple syrup
- Olive oil
- Light brown sugar

- Pepper
- Pure maple syrup
- Pure vanilla extract
- Red pepper flakes
- Red wine vinegar
- White wine vinegar
- Whole-grain mustard

WEEK 1

AT-A-GLANCE

MENU

DAY 1

BREAKFAST
2 Herbed Egg Bites

SNACK
2 slices sprouted grain bread

LUNCH
Chicken and Farro Salad

DINNER
Air Fryer Squash Soup

SNACK
1 serving multigrain pita chips + 2 Tbsp hummus

DAY 2

BREAKFAST
2 Herbed Egg Bites ❄

SNACK
1 large apple with cinnamon

LUNCH
Air Fryer Squash Soup 🥡 + grilled cheese

DINNER
Roasted White Fish with Cumin Roasted Tomatoes and Chickpeas

DESSERT
100-Calorie Greek Yogurt Ice Cream Bar

DAY 3

BREAKFAST
Oatmeal with Yogurt and Toasted Almonds

LUNCH
Roasted Chickpea, Tomato and Chicken Bowl 🍲

DINNER
Lemony Garlic and Herb Pork Tenderloin with Mushrooms and Kale

DAY 4

BREAKFAST
Jammy Egg Toast 🌓

LUNCH
Pork, Kale and Mushroom Pitas 🍲

DINNER
Mixed Pepper Pasta

DAY 5

BREAKFAST
Yogurt, Strawberry and Buckwheat Granola 🌓

LUNCH
Mixed Pepper Pasta 🥡

DINNER
Seared Steak with Blistered Tomatoes and Green Beans

DESSERT
3 pieces dark chocolate

DAY 6

BREAKFAST
Hot Honey Broiled Pineapple Toast

LUNCH
Steak, White Bean and Veggie Salad 🍲

DINNER
Air Fryer Salmon Flatbread

DAY 7

BREAKFAST
Turkish Eggs with Greek Yogurt

SNACK
2 slices sprouted grain bread

LUNCH
Scallion-Lemon Arugula Salad with Roasted Salmon 🍲

DINNER
Sheet Pan Roasted Chicken

DESSERT
3 pieces dark chocolate

🥡 Leftover = remainder of recipe that was eaten on a different day

🍲 Reinvented Leftover = ingredient was originally used in a different recipe

🍱 Meal Prepped = recipe fully prepped on a day other than the day it is eaten

🌓 Partially Prepped = part of the recipe is prepped on a day other than the day it is eaten

SHOPPING LIST

Buy just what you need each week. Below are exact amounts of every ingredient you will need for Week 1.

PRODUCE

1   small acorn squash (about 1 lb)
1   large apple
6   cups baby arugula
½   small avocado
2   cups baby greens (spinach, kale, arugula, or combination)
2½ lbs butternut squash
2   medium carrots
¾   cup chives
4   oz small cremini mushrooms
¾   cup fresh dill
1   bulb fennel
2½ cups flat-leaf parsley
1   Fresno chile
15 cloves garlic
2¾ pt grape tomatoes
½   lb green beans
1   small bunch green curly kale (about 8 oz)
1½ Tbsp mixed fresh herbs, such as parsley, mint, chives, rosemary and thyme
1   lemon
2½ cups mixed greens
1   large onion
1   orange
2   small peppers (red, yellow, orange or combination)
⅓   cup fresh pineapple chunks
3½ small red onions
3   scallions
¼   seedless cucumber
2½ small shallots
4   oz strawberries
11 sprigs fresh thyme

MEAT & SEAFOOD

2   6-oz chicken breasts
2   small bone-in chicken breasts (about 1½ lbs total)
5   oz firm white fish
1   10-oz pork tenderloin
1   10-oz skinless salmon fillet
1   1½-in.-thick strip steak (about 12 oz)

REFRIGERATED & DAIRY

1   Tbsp butter
2   slices cheese of choice
3   Tbsp cottage cheese
9   large eggs
½   oz feta, plus more for serving
¾   cup nonfat Greek yogurt
2   Tbsp hummus Mayonnaise, for serving
¼   cup milk
¼   cup orange juice
1   oz Romano cheese
¼   cup sour cream, plus more for serving

FROZEN

1   100-calorie Greek yogurt ice cream bar

BREAD & BAKERY

    Crusty bread, for serving
1   piece flatbread
6   slices sprouted grain bread
1   slice thick country bread
2   slices whole-grain bread
1   whole-wheat pita

PANTRY

½   cup sliced almonds
½   cup buckwheat groats
1   Tbsp capers
1   15-oz can chickpeas
½   Tbsp coriander seeds
1⅛ tsp cumin seeds
6   pieces dark chocolate
1   cup farro
1½ tsp fennel seeds
    Flaky salt, for serving
1   tsp hot honey
5   oz mezze rigatoni
1   serving multigrain pita chips
2   Tbsp pepitas
¼   cup quick-cooking steel-cut oats
⅓   cup red lentils
¼   tsp smoked paprika
½   tsp ground sumac
1½ Tbsp tomato paste
½   cup canned white beans
3   Tbsp white wine vinegar

SUNDAY PREP

ALMOND BUCKWHEAT GRANOLA (P. 44)

for Yogurt, Strawberry and
Buckwheat Granola (p. 96)

2/3 CUP DRY FARRO

for Chicken and Farro Salad
(p. 82) and Roasted Chickpea,
Tomato and Chicken Bowl (p. 88)

2 JAMMY EGGS

for Jammy Egg Toast (p. 92)

2 6-OZ BONELESS, SKINLESS CHICKEN BREASTS

for Chicken and Farro Salad
(p. 82) and Roasted Chickpea, Tomato
and Chicken Bowl (p. 88)

MEAL PLAN: Week 1

DAY 1

BREAKFAST

2 Herbed Egg Bites
(p. 40)

SNACK

2 slices sprouted grain bread

LUNCH

Chicken and Farro Salad
(p. 82)

DINNER

Air Fryer Squash Soup
(p. 60)
Refrigerate remaining in
airtight container for Day 2
lunch.

SNACK

1 serving multigrain pita
chips + 2 Tbsp hummus

NOTES TO SELF

WATER

MOVEMENT Y☐ N☐

ACTIVITY	DURATION	INTENSITY

SLEEP

Bedtime Last Night: _____ : _____
Wake Time This Morning: _____ : _____

MOOD

CONNECTION

MEAL PLAN: Week 1

DAY 2

BREAKFAST
2 Herbed Egg Bites 🗇
(p. 40)

SNACK
1 large apple with cinnamon

LUNCH
Air Fryer Squash Soup 🝫
(p. 60) + grilled cheese
(2 slices sprouted grain
bread, 1 Tbsp butter,
2 slices cheese of choice)

DINNER
Roasted White Fish
with Cumin Roasted
Tomatoes and Chickpeas
(p. 88)
Eat half the chickpeas and
tomatoes and refrigerate
the remaining in an
airtight container for
Day 3 lunch.

DESSERT
100-Calorie Greek Yogurt
Ice Cream Bar

NOTES TO SELF

WATER

MOVEMENT Y ☐ N ☐

ACTIVITY	DURATION	INTENSITY

SLEEP
Bedtime Last Night: _____ : _____
Wake Time This Morning: _____ : _____

MOOD

CONNECTION

DAY 3

BREAKFAST
Oatmeal with Yogurt and
Toasted Almonds (p. 86)

LUNCH
Roasted Chickpea, Tomato
and Chicken Bowl ♨
(p. 88)

DINNER
Lemony Garlic and Herb
Pork Tenderloin with
Mushrooms and Kale
(p. 90)
Refrigerate remaining in
airtight container for Day 4
lunch.

NOTES TO SELF

WATER

MOVEMENT Y☐ N☐

ACTIVITY	DURATION	INTENSITY

SLEEP
Bedtime Last Night: _____ : _____
Wake Time This Morning: _____ : _____

MOOD

CONNECTION

MEAL PLAN: Week 1

DAY 4

BREAKFAST
Jammy Egg Toast ⬤
(p. 92)

LUNCH
Pork, Kale and Mushroom
Pitas ♨ (p. 91)

DINNER
Mixed Pepper Pasta
(p. 94)
Refrigerate remaining in
airtight container for Day 5
lunch.

NOTES TO SELF

WATER

MOVEMENT Y ☐ N ☐

ACTIVITY	DURATION	INTENSITY

SLEEP
Bedtime Last Night: _____ : _____
Wake Time This Morning: _____ : _____

MOOD

CONNECTION

DAY 5

BREAKFAST

Yogurt, Strawberry and Buckwheat Granola ◖ (p. 96)

LUNCH

Mixed Pepper Pasta ◰ (p. 94)

DINNER

Seared Steak with Blistered Tomatoes and Green Beans (p. 98) Refrigerate remaining in airtight container for Day 6 lunch.

DESSERT

3 pieces dark chocolate

NOTES TO SELF

WATER

MOVEMENT Y☐ N☐

ACTIVITY	DURATION	INTENSITY

SLEEP

Bedtime Last Night: _____ : _____

Wake Time This Morning: _____ : _____

MOOD

CONNECTION

MEAL PLAN: Week 1

DAY 6

BREAKFAST
Hot Honey Broiled Pineapple Toast (p. 100)

LUNCH
Steak, White Bean and Veggie Salad ☺ (p. 102)

DINNER
Air Fryer Salmon Flatbread (p. 104)
Refrigerate remaining in airtight container for Day 7 lunch.

NOTES TO SELF

WATER

MOVEMENT Y ☐ N ☐

ACTIVITY	DURATION	INTENSITY

SLEEP
Bedtime Last Night: _____ : _____
Wake Time This Morning: _____ : _____

MOOD

CONNECTION

DAY 7

BREAKFAST
Turkish Eggs with Greek
Yogurt (p. 106)

SNACK
2 slices sprouted grain bread

LUNCH
Scallion-Lemon Arugula
Salad with Roasted Salmon
🍲 (p. 108)

DINNER
Sheet Pan Roasted Chicken
(p. 110)

DESSERT
3 pieces dark chocolate

NOTES TO SELF

WATER

MOVEMENT Y ☐ N ☐

ACTIVITY	DURATION	INTENSITY

SLEEP
Bedtime Last Night: _____ : _____
Wake Time This Morning: _____ : _____

MOOD

CONNECTION

WEEK 1
RECIPES

Chicken and Farro Salad

ACTIVE TIME 20 MIN. | TOTAL TIME 20 MIN.

⅛ small red onion,
   thinly sliced
1 Tbsp fresh lemon juice
   Kosher salt and pepper
1 cup cooked farro
½ Tbsp olive oil
1 Tbsp fresh dill, chopped
6 oz cooked chicken
   breast, sliced
½ cup grape tomatoes,
   halved
¼ seedless cucumber,
   cut into ½-in. pieces
1 cup baby arugula
½ small avocado, diced
½ oz feta, crumbled

1. In small bowl, toss onion with ½ Tbsp lemon juice and pinch salt. Let sit, tossing twice, for 10 min.

2. Toss farro with oil and remaining ½ Tbsp lemon juice, then dill. Fold in chicken, tomatoes, cucumber and onions (and their juices) and toss to combine. Fold in arugula, avocado and feta.

SERVES 1 *About 770 cal, 26 g fat (6 g sat), 66 g pro, 861 mg sodium, 79 g carb, 14 g fiber*

Roasted White Fish with Cumin Roasted Tomatoes and Chickpeas

ACTIVE TIME 15 MIN. | TOTAL TIME 30 MIN.

½ Tbsp coriander seeds
1   tsp cumin seeds
¼ tsp red pepper flakes
½ tsp ground sumac, divided
    Kosher salt and pepper
1   pint grape tomatoes
4   cloves garlic, smashed
2   Tbsp olive oil, divided
1   15-oz can chickpeas, rinsed
5   oz firm white fish
2   sprigs fresh thyme, leaves stripped

1. Heat oven to 425°F. With mortar and pestle, coarsely crush coriander and cumin seeds. Stir in red pepper flakes, ¼ tsp sumac and pinch salt.

2. On rimmed baking sheet, toss tomatoes and garlic with 1 Tbsp oil and spices. Roast 10 min.

3. Toss tomato mixture with chickpeas. Nestle fish in center, then drizzle with remaining Tbsp oil, season with remaining ¼ tsp sumac and ¼ tsp each salt and pepper, and sprinkle with thyme.

4. Roast until fish is just opaque throughout, about 15 min. depending on thickness. Serve fish with half veggies. Refrigerate remaining veggies in an airtight container for tomorrow.

SERVES 1 (WITH LEFTOVER VEGETABLES) *About 515 cal, 25 g fat (3 g sat), 34 g pro, 1,195 mg sodium, 49 g carb, 11 g fiber*

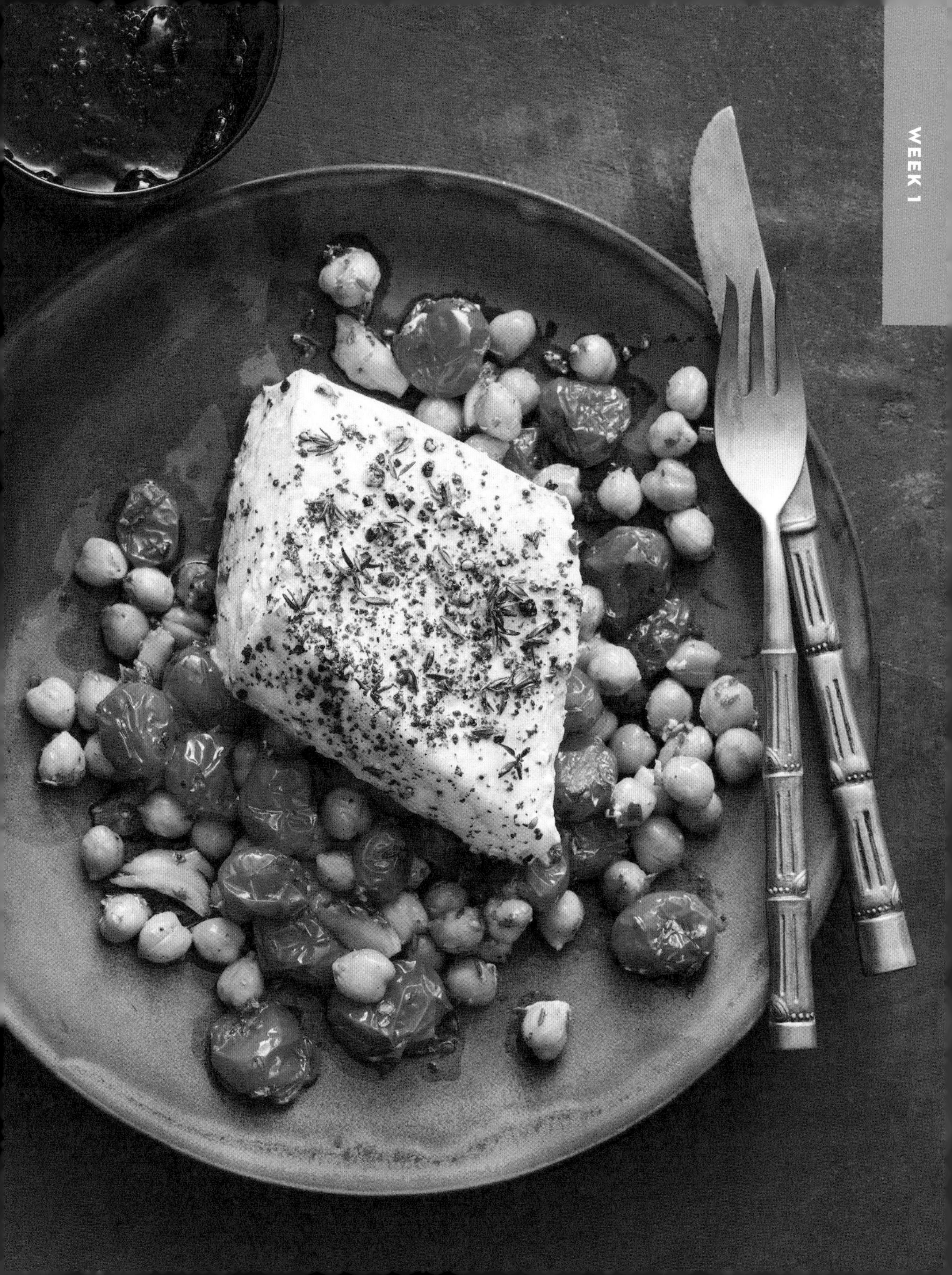

Oatmeal with Yogurt and Toasted Almonds

ACTIVE TIME 10 MIN. | TOTAL TIME 10 MIN.

½   cup water

¼   cup orange juice

¼   cup quick-cooking
     steel-cut oats

1½ Tbsp sliced almonds,
     toasted

1   tsp olive oil

2   Tbsp nonfat Greek yogurt
     Orange zest
     Aleppo pepper and flaky
     salt, for serving

1. In small saucepan, bring water and orange juice to boil. Add oats and cook, stirring occasionally, until tender, 5 to 7 min.

2. In small bowl, toss almonds with oil and pinch salt. Transfer oats to bowl, top with yogurt and almond mixture, then grate orange zest over top and sprinkle with Aleppo pepper and flaky salt, if desired.

SERVES 1 *About 305 cal, 12.5 g fat (1.5 g sat), 9 g pro, 125 mg sodium, 41 g carb, 5 g fiber*

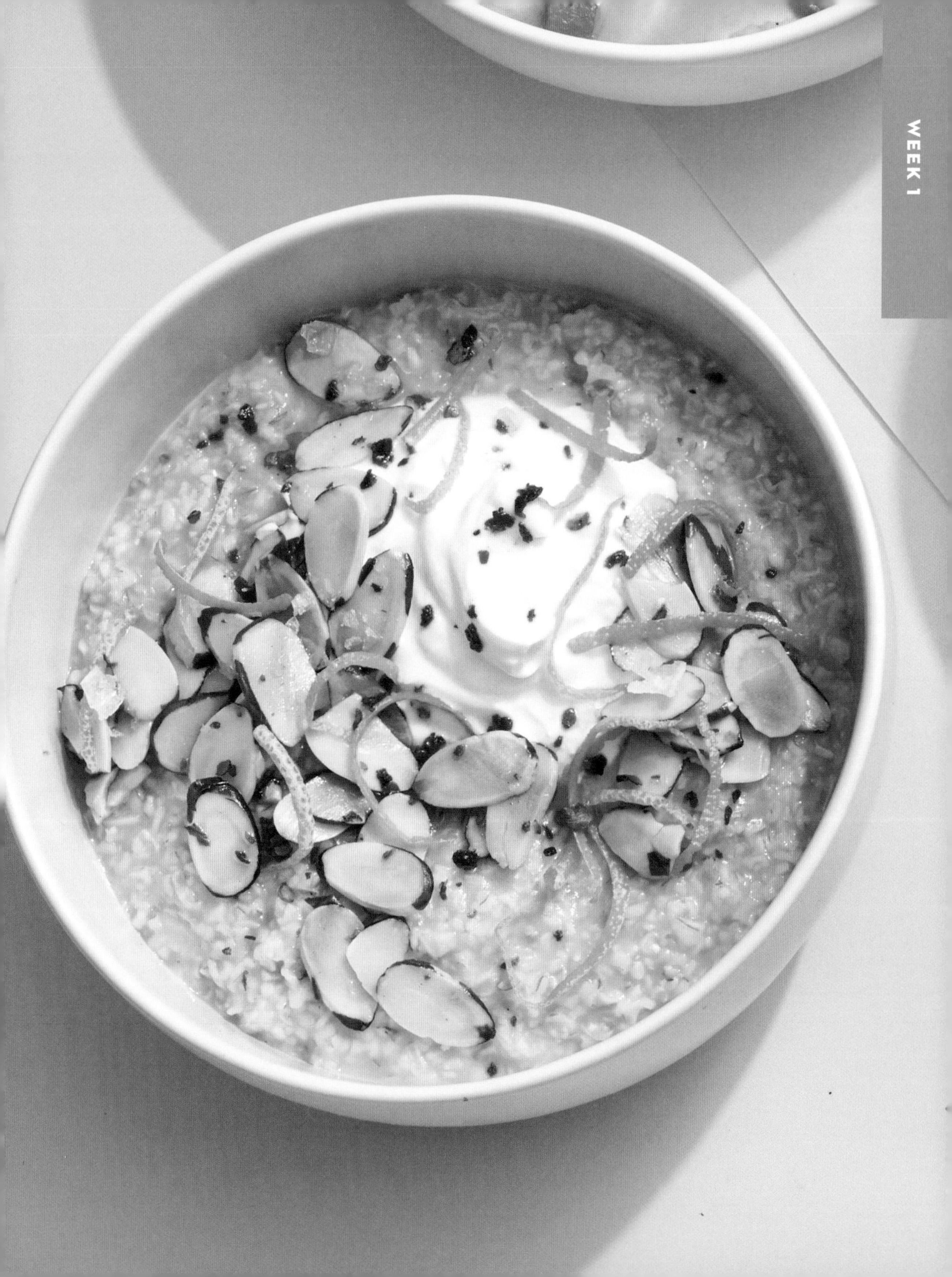

Roasted Chickpea, Tomato and Chicken Bowl

ACTIVE TIME 10 MIN. | TOTAL TIME 10 MIN.

½ cup cooked farro

½ scallion, thinly sliced

1 Tbsp white wine vinegar

½ Tbsp olive oil
    Kosher salt and pepper
    Leftover chickpeas and tomatoes from Roasted White Fish with Cumin Roasted Chickpeas and Tomatoes (p. 84)

4 oz cooked chicken breast, cut into pieces

2 cups baby greens (spinach, kale, arugula, or combination)

1. In bowl, toss farro, scallion, vinegar and oil and pinch each of salt and pepper. Fold in chickpea–tomato mixture and chicken, then greens.

SERVES 1 *About 630 cal, 21 g fat (3 g sat), 50 g pro, 1,095 mg sodium, 72 g carb, 16 g fiber*

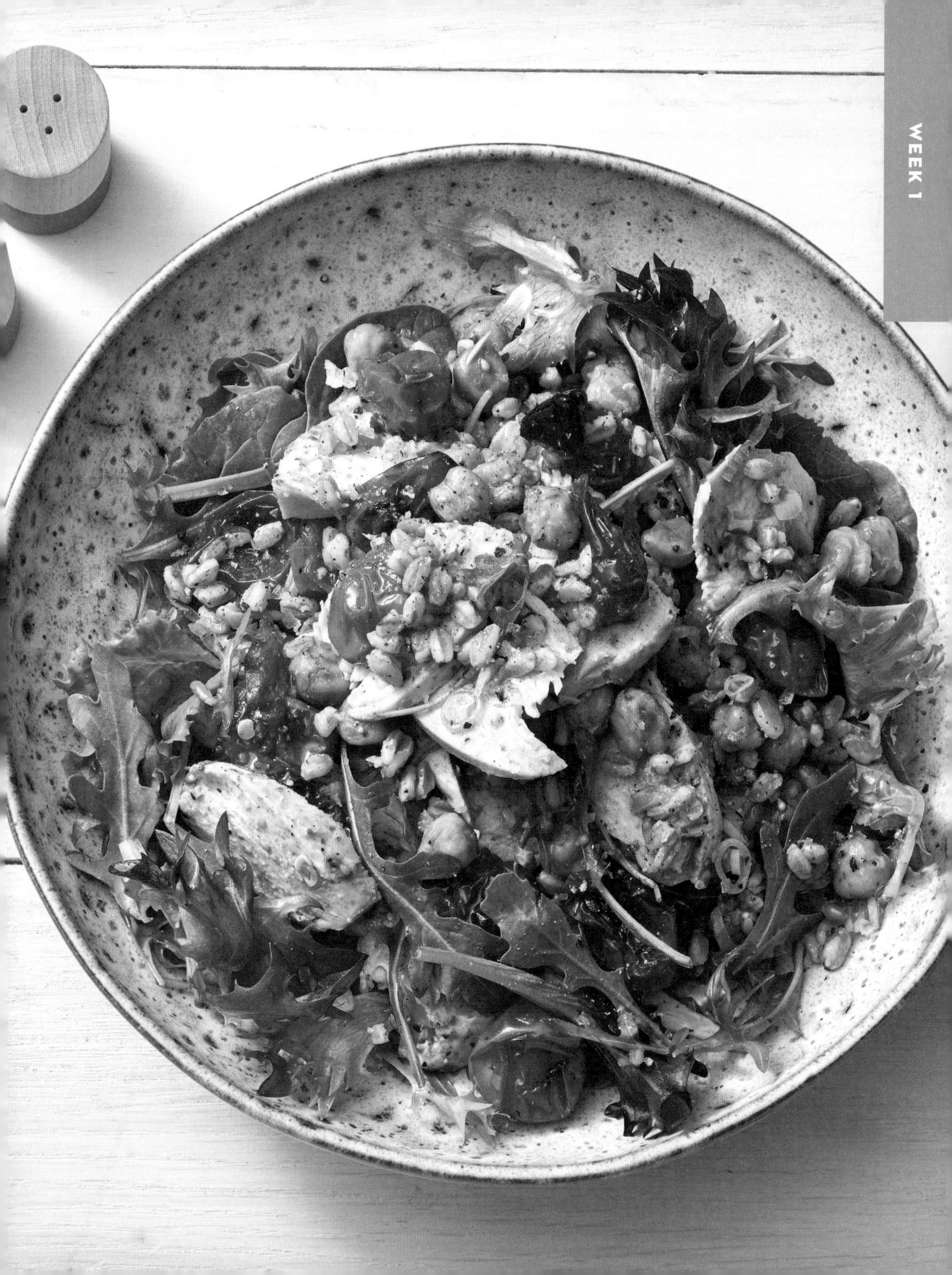

Lemony Garlic and Herb Pork Tenderloin with Mushrooms and Kale

ACTIVE TIME 30 MIN. | TOTAL TIME 30 MIN.

1½ Tbsp finely chopped mixed fresh herbs, such as parsley, mint, chives, rosemary and thyme

½ small clove garlic, finely grated

½ tsp grated lemon zest

⅛ red pepper flakes

3 Tbsp olive oil, divided

2 small shallots, peeled and halved
Kosher salt and pepper

1 10-oz pork tenderloin, halved crosswise

4 oz small cremini mushrooms, halved or quartered if large

1 small bunch green curly kale (8 oz), ribs removed, leaves torn into large pieces

1. In small bowl, combine herbs, garlic, lemon zest, red pepper flakes and 1 Tbsp oil.

2. Heat air fryer to 400°F. In large bowl, toss shallots with ½ Tbsp oil and pinch each salt and pepper. Season pork with ¼ tsp salt. Transfer shallots and pork to air fryer and air-fry 5 min.

3. Brush herb mixture over top and sides of pork, flip shallots and continue air-frying 5 min.

4. While pork and shallots are cooking, in same large bowl, toss mushrooms with ½ Tbsp oil and pinch each salt and pepper. Add mushrooms to air fryer (with shallots and pork) and air-fry until pork registers 145°F on instant-read thermometer and mushrooms and shallots are golden brown and tender, 5 to 7 min. more. Transfer pork to cutting board and let rest at least 10 min. before slicing. Transfer vegetables to plate.

5. In same large bowl, toss kale with remaining 1 Tbsp oil and pinch salt and pepper, add to air fryer basket and cook until kale has wilted and has slightly crispy edges, 3 min. Return mushrooms and shallots to air fryer and toss to combine. Transfer one-third veggie mixture to container and refrigerate for lunch tomorrow. Slice half pork and serve with remaining vegetables. Refrigerate remaining pork with reserved vegetables for tomorrow.

SERVES 2 *About 668 cal, 52 g fat (8 g sat), 36 g pro, 593 mg sodium, 20 g carb, 7 g fiber*

REINVENTED LEFTOVER: LUNCH

Pork, Kale and Mushroom Pitas

ACTIVE TIME 10 MIN. | TOTAL TIME 10 MIN.

1   whole-wheat pita, toasted
1½   Tbsp nonfat Greek yogurt
¼   small scallion, finely chopped
¼   tsp lemon zest
4   oz leftover pork from
    Lemony Garlic and
    Herb Pork Tenderloin
    (p. 90), sliced
    Leftover Mushrooms
    and Kale (p. 90)

1. Split pita and spread inside with yogurt. Sprinkle with scallion and lemon zest, then stuff with leftover sliced pork, mushrooms and kale.

SERVES 1 *About 640 cal, 34 g fat (6 g sat), 41 g pro, 790 mg sodium, 47 g carb, 8 g fiber*

WEEK 1

Jammy Egg Toast

ACTIVE TIME 10 MIN. | TOTAL TIME 10 MIN.

1   Tbsp white wine vinegar
½   small shallot, finely
       chopped
¼   tsp fresh thyme, plus
       more for sprinkling
       Kosher salt and pepper
½   Tbsp olive oil
1   tsp whole-grain mustard
½   Tbsp chopped parsley, plus
       more for sprinkling
1   thick slice country bread,
       toasted
       Mayonnaise, for serving
2   Jammy Eggs (p. 42),
       peeled

1. In small bowl, combine vinegar, shallot, thyme and pinch each salt and pepper. Let sit, tossing occasionally, 10 min.

2. Stir oil, mustard and parsley into shallot mixture. Spread bread with mayo, then coarsely chop eggs and arrange on top of bread. Spoon shallot vinaigrette over top and sprinkle with more thyme, parsley and cracked pepper if desired.

SERVES 1 *About 317 cal, 17 g fat (4 g sat), 16 g pro, 730 mg sodium, 24 g carb, 2 g fiber*

Mixed Pepper Pasta

ACTIVE TIME 25 MIN. | TOTAL TIME 25 MIN.

2 Tbsp olive oil, divided
2 small peppers (red, yellow,
   orange, or combination),
   cut in 1/2-in. pieces
1 red onion, chopped
1/2 tsp red pepper flakes
   Kosher salt
1 large clove garlic, finely
   chopped
1 1/2 tsp fennel seeds
1 1/2 Tbsp tomato paste
5 oz mezze rigatoni
1/3 cup red lentils
3 3/4 cups water
1 oz Romano cheese, grated

1. In large skillet on medium, heat 1/2 Tbsp oil. Add peppers and onion, season with red pepper flakes and 1/4 tsp salt and cook, tossing occasionally, until just tender, about 6 min. Transfer to bowl.

2. Add remaining 1 1/2 Tbsp oil to skillet along with garlic and fennel seeds and cook, stirring for 1 min. Stir in tomato paste and cook 1 min. Add pasta, lentils, water and 1/4 tsp salt and simmer, stirring often, until pasta is just tender, 12 to 15 min.

3. Toss with Romano until melted and a thick sauce is created, then fold in pepper-onion mixture. Serve half of pasta for dinner and reserve remaining pasta for lunch tomorrow.

SERVES 2 *About 600 cal, 19 g fat (4.5 g sat), 23 g pro, 665 mg sodium, 85 g carb, 10 g fiber*

Yogurt, Strawberry and Buckwheat Granola

ACTIVE TIME 10 MIN. | TOTAL TIME 10 MIN.

4   oz (½ cup) strawberries, sliced
½   tsp pure maple syrup
⅓   cup nonfat Greek yogurt
3   Tbsp Almond Buckwheat Granola (p. 44)

1. In bowl, toss strawberries and maple syrup to coat; let sit 5 min.

2. Spoon yogurt into bowl. Toss strawberries again, then spoon over yogurt with any juices and top with granola.

SERVES 1 *About 195 cal, 8 g fat (1 g sat), 11 g pro, 180 mg sodium, 23 g carb, 4 g fiber*

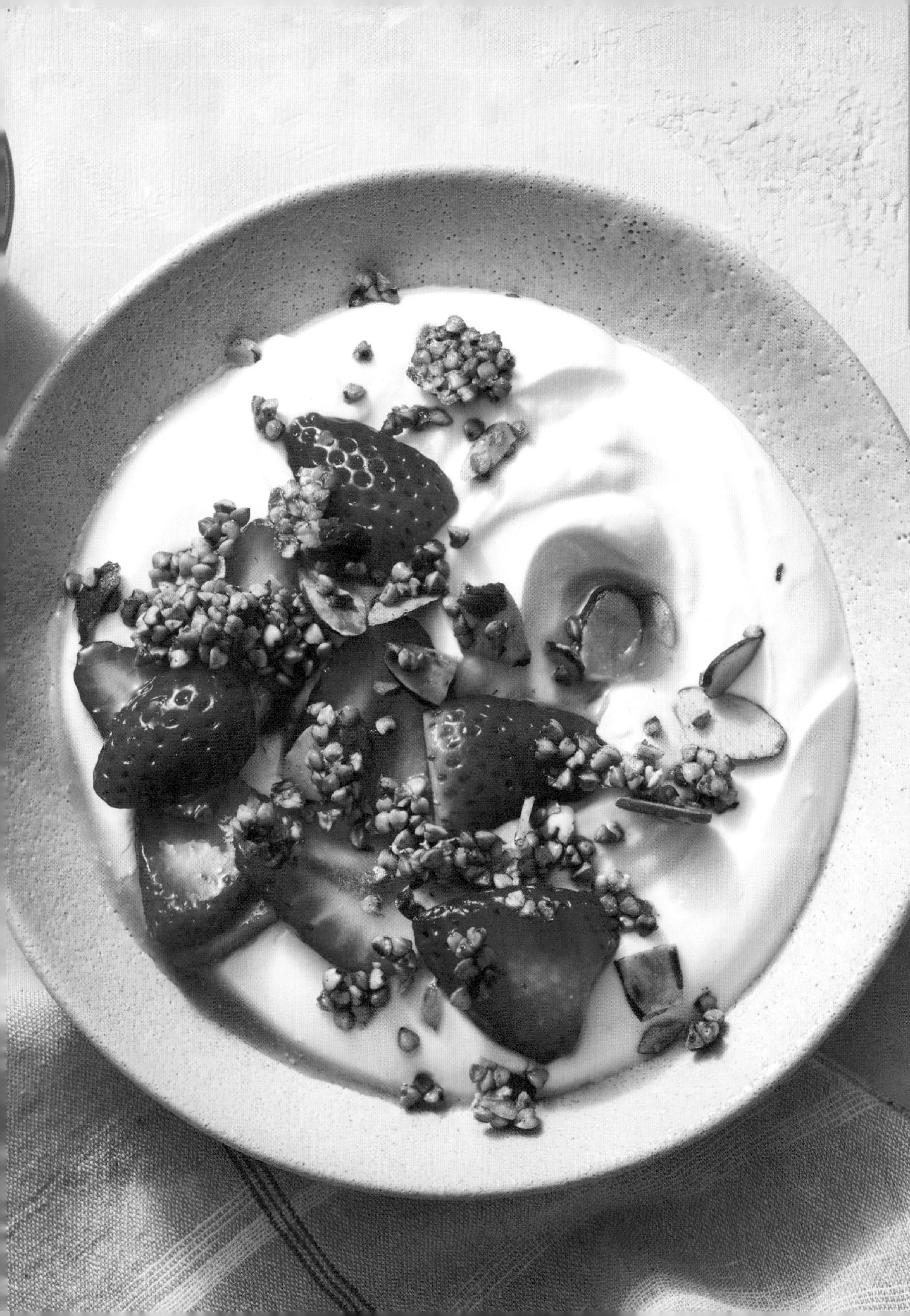

Seared Steak with Blistered Tomatoes and Green Beans

ACTIVE TIME 25 MIN. | TOTAL TIME 25 MIN. PLUS RESTING

½ lb green beans

1 pint grape tomatoes

2 Tbsp plus 1 tsp olive oil
   Kosher salt and pepper

1 1½-in. thick strip steak
   (about 12 oz), trimmed

4 cloves garlic (in skins)

1 Tbsp white wine vinegar

¼ small red onion, finely
   chopped

1. Heat oven to 450°F. On large rimmed baking sheet, toss together green beans and tomatoes with 1 Tbsp oil and pinch each salt and pepper. Roast until vegetables are tender and beginning to brown, 10 to 12 min.

2. Meanwhile, in medium cast-iron skillet on medium, heat tsp oil. Season steak with ¼ tsp each salt and pepper, add steak to skillet along with garlic and cook until browned, 3 min. per side. Transfer skillet to oven along with vegetables and roast to desired doneness, 3 to 4 min. for medium-rare. Transfer to cutting board and let rest at least 5 min. before slicing half.

3. In small bowl, combine vinegar, remaining Tbsp oil and pinch each salt and pepper; stir in onion. Serve sliced steak with half of the green beans and tomatoes and spoon half vinegar-onion mixture over top. Refrigerate remaining vegetables, steak and marinated onions for lunch tomorrow.

SERVES 2 *About 565 cal, 37 g fat (11 g sat), 41 g pro, 455 mg sodium, 17 g carb, 5 g fiber*

Hot Honey Broiled Pineapple Toast

ACTIVE TIME 10 MIN. | TOTAL TIME 10 MIN. PLUS RESTING

1   tsp olive oil
⅓   cup fresh pineapple chunks
1   tsp hot honey plus more
    for serving
1   slice whole-grain bread,
    toasted
3   Tbsp cottage cheese
    Aleppo pepper,
    for sprinkling

1. Place oven rack on highest level and heat broiler.

2. Meanwhile, grease small rimmed baking sheet with oil. Place pineapple chunks on top, drizzle with hot honey and toss to combine. Arrange in single layer and broil, 1½ min. Toss and continue broiling until golden brown, 1½ min. more.

3. Top toast with cottage cheese and spoon pineapple on top. Drizzle with additional honey and sprinkle with Aleppo pepper if desired.

SERVES 1 *About 255 cal, 7 g fat (2 g sat), 10 g pro, 315 mg sodium, 39 g carb, 4 g fiber*

Steak, White Bean and Veggie Salad

ACTIVE TIME 15 MIN. | TOTAL TIME 15 MIN.

Leftover vinegar-onion mixture from Seared Steak with Blistered Tomatoes and Green Beans (p. 98)

½ cup canned white beans, rinsed

3 cups mixed greens
Leftover steak from Seared Steak with Blistered Tomatoes and Green Beans (p. 98), cut into pieces
Leftover tomatoes and green beans from Seared Steak with Blistered Tomatoes and Green Beans (p. 98)

1. In bowl, toss vinegar-onion mixture with white beans. Toss with beans, greens and leftover steak, green beans and tomatoes.

SERVES 1 *About 707 cal, 38 g fat (11 g sat), 51 g pro, 620 mg sodium, 42 g carb, 17 g fiber*

Air Fryer Salmon Flatbread

ACTIVE TIME 15 MIN. | TOTAL TIME 15 MIN.

1   Tbsp red wine vinegar
2   Tbsp olive oil, divided
1   Tbsp capers, chopped
2   scallions, 1 finely chopped
     and 1 thinly sliced
     Kosher salt and pepper
1   pint grape tomatoes
10   oz skinless salmon fillet,
     cut into 1½-in. pieces
1   Tbsp chopped flat-leaf
     parsley
     Nonfat Greek yogurt,
     for serving
1   piece flatbread, warmed
2   cups baby arugula
     Crumbled feta, for serving

1. In small bowl, combine red wine vinegar, 1 Tbsp olive oil, capers, chopped scallion and ¼ tsp pepper; set aside.

2. Heat air fryer to 400°F. In bowl, toss tomatoes and remaining Tbsp oil with ¼ tsp each salt and pepper. Season salmon with ¼ tsp each salt and pepper.

3. Place salmon in single layer on 1 side of air fryer and add tomatoes to remaining space (piling them is great). Air-fry until salmon is just barely opaque throughout, 6 min.

4. Transfer tomatoes to bowl with vinegar–scallion mixture and toss to combine, then toss with parsley.

5. Transfer ½ salmon and ½ tomato mixture to container to use for lunch tomorrow.

6. Spread yogurt on flatbread, top with remaining salmon and arugula, then spoon tomato mixture on top. Sprinkle with sliced scallions and crumbled feta if desired.

SERVES 1 (WITH LEFTOVER SALMON AND TOMATOES)
About 680 cal, 35 g fat (12 g sat), 47 g pro, 1,341 mg sodium, 51 g carb, 5 g fiber

Turkish Eggs with Greek Yogurt

ACTIVE TIME 15 MIN. | TOTAL TIME 15 MIN.

⅓ cup nonfat Greek yogurt,
     at room temperature
2 Tbsp dill, chopped,
     plus more for serving
¼ tsp grated garlic
     Kosher salt
1 Tbsp olive oil
½ tsp Aleppo pepper,
     plus more for serving
⅛ tsp cumin seeds
1 large egg
     Flaked salt
     Toast, for serving

1. In small bowl, combine Greek yogurt, dill, garlic and pinch salt.

2. In small nonstick skillet, heat olive oil on medium until warm. Remove from heat, stir in Aleppo pepper and cumin seeds, and let sit 4 min. Spoon half of oil into a small bowl and reserve.

3. Return skillet with remaining oil to medium heat and cook egg to desired doneness, about 2 min. for a runny yolk.

4. Spread yogurt onto plate. Top with egg, reserved oil and dill. Sprinkle with additional Aleppo pepper and flaked salt if desired and serve with toast.

SERVES 1 *About 240 cal, 19 g fat (3.5 g sat), 14 g pro, 290 mg sodium, 4 g carb, 0 g fiber*

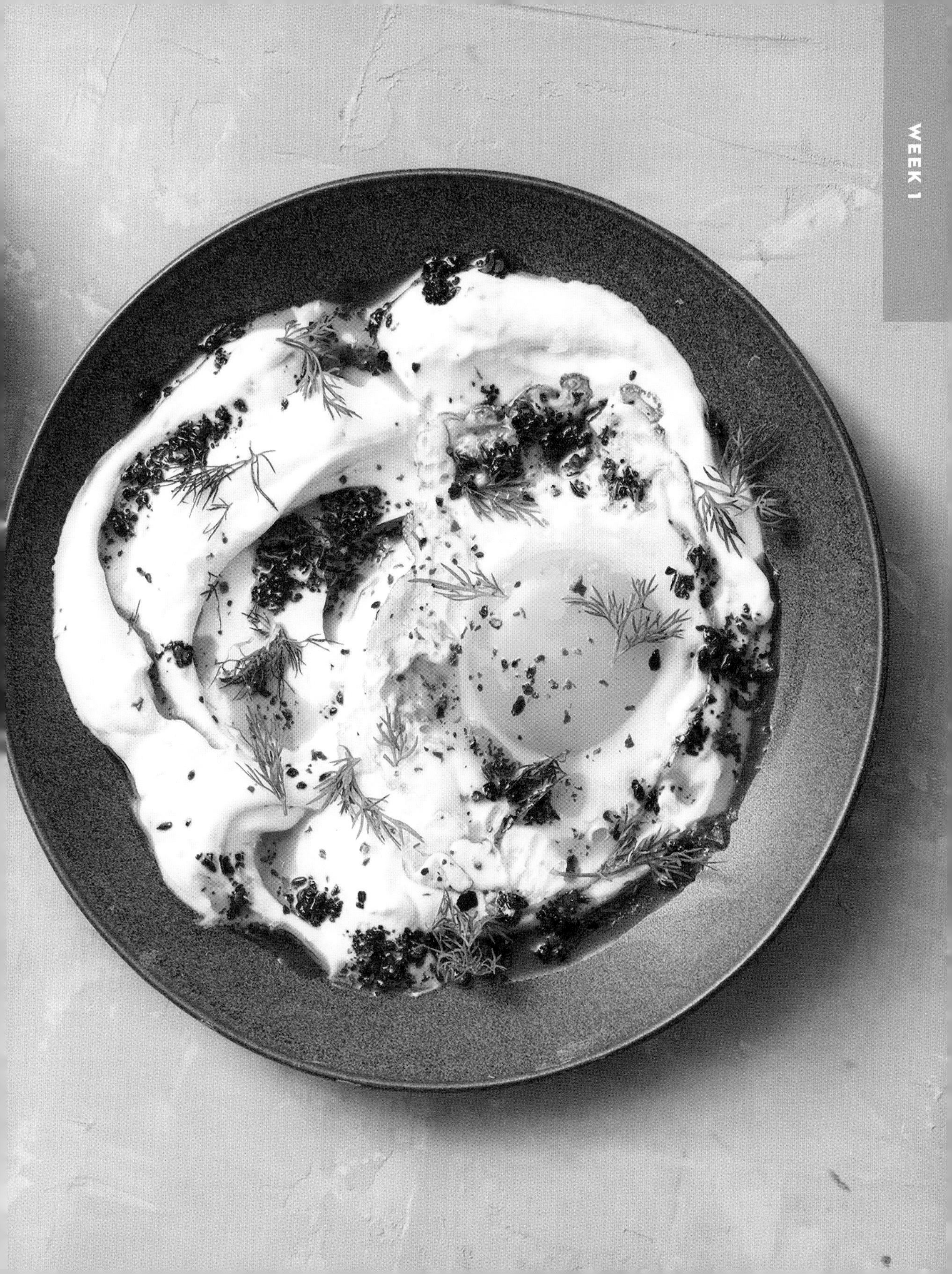

Scallion-Lemon Arugula Salad with Roasted Salmon

ACTIVE TIME 10 MIN. | TOTAL TIME 10 MIN.

½ Tbsp olive oil

½ Tbsp lemon juice

¼ tsp honey

Kosher salt and pepper

3 cups baby arugula

Leftover tomatoes from
Air Fryer Salmon Flatbread
(p. 104)

Leftover salmon from
Air Fryer Salmon Flatbread
(p. 104)

1. In large bowl, whisk together oil, lemon juice, honey and pinch each salt and pepper until dissolved. Toss with arugula and serve with tomatoes and salmon.

SERVES 1 *About 455 cal, 27 g fat (4 g sat), 39 g pro, 850 mg sodium, 23 g carb, 4 g fiber*

Sheet Pan Roasted Chicken

ACTIVE TIME 20 MIN. | TOTAL TIME 45 MIN.

2 small red onions, cut into ½-in.-thick wedges

1 small acorn squash (about 1 lb), cut into ¾-in.-thick wedges

1 bulb fennel, cut into ½-in.-thick wedges

1 Tbsp plus 2 tsp olive oil

4 sprigs fresh thyme, divided, plus more for serving
    Kosher salt and pepper

2 small bone-in chicken breasts (about 1½ lbs total)

1. Heat oven to 425°F. On a rimmed baking sheet, toss vegetables with 1 Tbsp oil, thyme and ¼ tsp each salt and pepper and roast 15 min.

2. Meanwhile, heat remaining 2 tsp oil in medium skillet on medium. Season chicken with ¼ tsp each salt and pepper and cook, skin side down until deep golden brown, 8 to 10 min. Flip and cook 3 min. more.

3. Nestle chicken among vegetables and roast until chicken is cooked through, 15 to 18 min. more. Transfer chicken to cutting board and let rest at least 5 min. before slicing.

4. Return vegetables to oven, while chicken is resting and roast until ready to serve (should be about 5 min. more). Transfer ⅓ of vegetables to plate. Slice half chicken and serve with vegetables and sprinkle with additional thyme, if desired. Refrigerate leftover chicken and vegetables for lunch next week.

SERVES 1 (WITH LEFTOVER CHICKEN AND VEGETABLES)
About 460 cal, 21 g fat (5 g sat), 33 g pro, 620 mg sodium, 38 g carb, 8 g fiber

AT-A-GLANCE

MENU

DAY 8

BREAKFAST
Zucchini Bread

LUNCH
Kale Salad with Chicken and Vegetables ♨

DINNER
Tomato, White Bean and Vegetable Soup + 2 slices sprouted grain bread

DESSERT
100-Calorie Greek Yogurt Ice Cream Bar

DAY 9

BREAKFAST
Citrus-Spiced Overnight Oats 🍱

LUNCH
Bulgur with Roasted Vegetables and Feta Dressing ♨

DINNER
Seared Chicken with Cheesy Spinach and Artichokes

DESSERT
3 pieces dark chocolate

DAY 10

BREAKFAST
Scrambled Egg Toast with Tomato and Parmesan

LUNCH
Chicken, Spinach and Artichoke Wraps ♨

DINNER
Sautéed Fish with Tomatoes and Capers

DESSERT
1 large apple with cinnamon

DAY 11

BREAKFAST
Zucchini Bread 🍱

LUNCH
Tomato, White Bean and Vegetable Soup 🍱 + 2 slices sprouted grain bread

DINNER
Aleppo Grilled Steak with Farro Salad
1 cup steamed asparagus

DAY 12

BREAKFAST
Apricot Pistachio Oatmeal Bowl

LUNCH
Open-Faced Steak and Arugula Sandwich ♨

DINNER
Balsamic Chicken and Onion Salad

DESSERT
100-Calorie Greek Yogurt Ice Cream Bar

DAY 13

BREAKFAST
Smoked Salmon Omelet + 2 slices sprouted grain bread

LUNCH
Bulgur with Chicken and Onion ♨ + 1 cup steamed asparagus

DINNER
Pepper and Onion Pizza 🍱

DESSERT
100-Calorie Greek Yogurt Ice Cream Bar

DAY 14

BREAKFAST
2 Buckwheat and Fig Muffins

LUNCH
Chickpea Salad Sandwich

DINNER
Lamb Chops and Snap Pea Salad

DESSERT
1 large apple with cinnamon

🍱 Leftover
♨ Reinvented Leftover
🍱 Meal Prepped
🍲 Partially Prepped

SHOPPING LIST

Below are exact amounts of everything you will need for Week 2. Be sure to check for leftovers from Week 1 before purchasing items from this list.

PRODUCE

2 large apples
1 small bunch arugula
2 cups asparagus
3 cups baby kale
2 cups baby spinach or kale
1/4 cup small basil leaves
6 oz Campari tomatoes
2 medium carrots
4 Castelvetrano olives
2 stalks celery
1/2 Tbsp fresh chives
2 small bulbs fennel
16 fresh figs
1 1/2 cups flat-leaf parsley
3 cloves garlic
1 head Gem lettuce
1/2 cup grape tomatoes
4 oz green beans
2 leaves green leaf lettuce
1 small jalapeño
3 kalamata olives
2 lemons
3/4 cup fresh mint
1 large onion
1 small onion
1 small orange
1 Persian cucumber or 1/4 seedless cucumber
1 poblano pepper
  Pomegranate arils, for serving
4 small radishes
2 medium red onions
1 small red onion
1 small red pepper

1/2 scallion
1 small shallot
1 small bunch spinach
1/2 cup sprouts
6 oz sugar snap peas
8 sprigs fresh thyme
1 small tomato
1/2 cup watercress
1 small yellow pepper
1/2 lb small zucchini (about 2)

MEAT & SEAFOOD

4 6-oz boneless, skinless chicken breasts
1/2 rack lamb (4 to 5 bones total)
1 6-oz skinless cod fillet
1 1/2 oz smoked salmon
1 12-oz strip steak (about 1 1/2 in. thick)

REFRIGERATED & DAIRY

1/2 cup cashew milk, plus more for serving
1/2 oz extra-sharp Cheddar
7 large eggs
1 oz feta
3 Tbsp Garlic & Fine Herbs Boursin
  Crumbled goat cheese, for serving
1 Tbsp nonfat Greek yogurt
2 Tbsp low-fat milk
1 Tbsp vegan mayonnaise
1/4 cup milk
3/4 cup orange juice
1 small wedge Parmesan
1 lb pizza dough
1 cup plain full-fat yogurt

FROZEN

3 100-calorie Greek yogurt ice cream bars

BREAD & BAKERY

6 slices sprouted grain bread
6 slices whole-grain bread
1 whole-wheat tortilla or sandwich wrap

PANTRY

1/2 tsp Aleppo pepper
1 14-oz can artichoke halves
1 1/4 tsp avocado oil
3 Tbsp balsamic vinegar
1 cup buckwheat flour
2/3 cup bulgur
1 tsp capers
  Pinch of cardamom
1/2 Tbsp chia seeds
1 Tbsp chicken or vegetable base (optional)
1 15-oz can low-sodium chickpeas
1 tsp whole coriander
  Cornmeal, for baking sheet
3 pieces dark chocolate
2 dried apricots
1/3 cup quick-cooking farro
1/2 Tbsp nutritional yeast
1/2 cup oat flour
1 1/2 Tbsp pistachios
1 1/2 Tbsp rice vinegar
6 Tbsp rolled oats
4 oz short pasta
1/4 cup quick-cooking steel-cut oats
1/2 tsp ground sumac
1/2 Tbsp tahini

1 28-oz can whole peeled tomatoes
1 1/8 Tbsp walnuts
2 15-oz cans white beans (cannellini, navy, butter, or a combination)

ALCOHOL

1/4 cup dry rosé or white wine
3/4 cup dry white wine

SUNDAY PREP

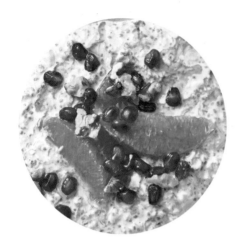

CITRUS-SPICED OVERNIGHT OATS (P. 48)

⅓ CUP BULGUR (P. 34)

for Bulgur with Roasted Vegetables and Feta Dressing (p. 125) and Bulgur with Chicken and Onion (p. 139)

TOMATO, WHITE BEAN AND VEGETABLE SOUP (P. 62)

MEAL PLAN: Week 2

DAY 8

BREAKFAST
Zucchini Bread (p. 46)
Store in airtight container for
Day 11 breakfast.

LUNCH
Kale Salad with Chicken and
Vegetables 🥣 (p. 124)

DINNER
Tomato, White Bean and
Vegetable Soup (p. 62) +
2 slices sprouted grain bread
Refrigerate remaining soup
in airtight container for Day
9 lunch.

DESSERT
100-Calorie Greek Yogurt
Ice Cream Bar

NOTES TO SELF

WATER

MOVEMENT Y☐ N☐

ACTIVITY	DURATION	INTENSITY

SLEEP
Bedtime Last Night: _____ : _____
Wake Time This Morning: _____ : _____

MOOD

CONNECTION

MEAL PLAN: Week 2

DAY 9

BREAKFAST

Citrus-Spiced
Overnight Oats ▢ (p. 48)

LUNCH

Bulgur with Roasted
Vegetables and Feta
Dressing ♨ (p. 125)

DINNER

Seared Chicken with
Cheesy Spinach and
Artichokes (p. 126)
Refrigerate remaining
chicken for Day 10 lunch.

DESSERT

3 pieces dark chocolate

NOTES TO SELF

WATER

MOVEMENT Y☐ N☐

ACTIVITY	DURATION	INTENSITY

SLEEP

Bedtime Last Night: _____ : _____
Wake Time This Morning: _____ : _____

MOOD

CONNECTION

DAY 10

BREAKFAST
Scrambled Egg Toast
with Tomato and Parmesan
(p. 128)

LUNCH
Chicken, Spinach and
Artichoke Wraps ♨
(p. 127)

DINNER
Sautéed Fish with
Tomatoes and Capers
(p. 130)

DESSERT
1 large apple with
cinnamon

NOTES TO SELF

WATER

MOVEMENT Y☐ N☐

ACTIVITY	DURATION	INTENSITY

SLEEP
Bedtime Last Night: _____ : _____
Wake Time This Morning: _____ : _____

MOOD

CONNECTION

MEAL PLAN: Week 2

DAY 11

BREAKFAST

Zucchini Bread 🍽 (p. 46)

LUNCH

Tomato, White Bean and Vegetable Soup 🍽 (p. 62) + 2 slices sprouted grain bread

DINNER

Aleppo Grilled Steak with Farro Salad (p. 132)

1 cup steamed asparagus

NOTES TO SELF

WATER

MOVEMENT Y ☐ N ☐

ACTIVITY	DURATION	INTENSITY

SLEEP

Bedtime Last Night: _____ : _____

Wake Time This Morning: _____ : _____

MOOD

CONNECTION

DAY 12

BREAKFAST
Apricot Pistachio Oatmeal
Bowl (p. 134)

LUNCH
Open-Faced Steak
and Arugula
Sandwich ♨ (p. 136)

DINNER
Balsamic Chicken and
Onion Salad (p. 138)

DESSERT
100-Calorie Greek Yogurt
Ice Cream Bar

WATER

MOVEMENT Y ☐ N ☐

ACTIVITY	DURATION	INTENSITY

SLEEP

Bedtime Last Night: _____ : _____

Wake Time This Morning: _____ : _____

NOTES TO SELF

MOOD

CONNECTION

MEAL PLAN: Week 2

DAY 13

WEEK 2

BREAKFAST
Smoked Salmon
Omelet (p. 140) + 2 slices
sprouted grain bread

LUNCH
Bulgur with Chicken and
Onion ♨ (p. 139) + 1 cup
steamed asparagus

DINNER
Pepper and Onion
Pizza ▣ (p. 64)

DESSERT
100-Calorie Greek Yogurt
Ice Cream Bar

NOTES TO SELF

WATER

MOVEMENT   Y☐ N☐

ACTIVITY	DURATION	INTENSITY

SLEEP

Bedtime Last Night: _____ : _____

Wake Time This Morning: _____ : _____

MOOD

CONNECTION

DAY 14

BREAKFAST

2 Buckwheat and
Fig Muffins (p. 50)
Freeze remaining in airtight
container for Day 18
breakfast.

LUNCH

Chickpea Salad
Sandwich (p. 142)

DINNER

Lamb Chops and Snap Pea
Salad (p. 144)

DESSERT

1 large apple with
cinnamon

NOTES TO SELF

WATER

MOVEMENT Y ☐ N ☐

ACTIVITY	DURATION	INTENSITY

SLEEP

Bedtime Last Night: _____ : _____

Wake Time This Morning: _____ : _____

MOOD

CONNECTION

WEEK 2
RECIPES

Kale Salad with Chicken and Vegetables

ACTIVE TIME 15 MIN. | TOTAL TIME 15 MIN.

½ Tbsp olive oil

2 tsp red wine vinegar

¼ tsp Dijon mustard
Kosher salt and pepper

3 cups baby kale
Leftover chicken breast from Sheet Pan Roasted Chicken (p. 110), sliced

2 wedges leftover acorn squash from Sheet Pan Roasted Chicken (p. 110)

2 wedges leftover roasted red onion from Sheet Pan Roasted Chicken (p. 110), halved

2 wedges leftover roasted fennel from Sheet Pan Roasted Chicken (p. 110), roughly chopped
Crumbled goat cheese, for serving

1. In large bowl, whisk together oil, vinegar, mustard and pinch each salt and pepper.

2. Toss dressing with kale then chicken and vegetables. Serve topped with goat cheese, if desired.

SERVES 1 *About 490 cal, 25.5 g fat (5.5 g sat), 35 g pro, 660 mg sodium, 32 g carb, 9 g fiber*

REINVENTED LEFTOVER: LUNCH

Bulgur with Roasted Vegetables and Feta Dressing

ACTIVE TIME 10 MIN. | TOTAL TIME 10 MIN.

2   Tbsp low-fat milk
1   oz feta, crumbled
½   Tbsp fresh lemon juice
¼   tsp lemon zest
     Kosher salt and pepper
1   cup bulgur, cooked
3   wedges leftover roasted red onions from Sheet Pan Roasted Chicken (p. 110), chopped
2   wedges leftover roasted fennel from Sheet Pan Roasted Chicken (p. 110), chopped
2   cups baby spinach or kale, chopped

1. In mini food processor, puree milk, feta, lemon juice, zest, salt and pepper until smooth.

2. In a bowl, toss bulgur, onions and fennel, then fold in spinach and top with feta dressing.

SERVES 1 *About 395 cal, 18 g fat (7 g sat), 14 g pro, 495 mg sodium, 49 g carb, 13 g fiber*

Seared Chicken with Cheesy Spinach and Artichokes

ACTIVE TIME 25 MIN. | TOTAL TIME 30 MIN.

2   Tbsp olive oil, divided
1   14-oz can artichoke halves,
    patted dry
    Kosher salt and pepper
2   6-oz boneless, skinless
    chicken breasts, pounded
    to ½-in. thick
¼   cup dry white wine
3   Tbsp Garlic & Fine Herbs
    Boursin
1   small bunch spinach,
    thick stems discarded,
    roughly chopped

1. In a large skillet on medium-high, heat 1 Tbsp oil. Add artichoke halves, cut sides down, and pinch each of salt and pepper and cook until golden brown, 3 min. Transfer to a plate.

2. Reduce heat to medium and add remaining Tbsp oil to the skillet. Season chicken breasts with ¼ tsp each salt and pepper, place in skillet and cook until golden brown and cooked through, 5 to 7 min. per side. Transfer to plate.

3. Remove skillet from heat, add wine and cook, scraping up any browned bits, 2 min. Stir in Garlic & Fine Herbs Boursin until melted. Return to heat and fold in spinach to wilt. Fold in artichokes.

4. Transfer 1 chicken breast and ½ spinach mixture to a container for lunch the following day. Serve remaining chicken with remaining spinach mixture.

SERVES 2 *About 540 cal, 31 g fat (10 g sat), 46 g pro, 820 mg sodium, 20 g carb, 9 g fiber*

REINVENTED LEFTOVER: LUNCH

Chicken, Spinach and Artichoke Wrap

ACTIVE TIME 10 MIN. | TOTAL TIME 10 MIN.

Leftover chicken from Seared Chicken with Cheesy Spinach and Artichoke (p. 126), shredded

Leftover cheesy spinach and artichoke from Seared Chicken with Cheesy Spinach and Artichoke (p. 126), roughly chopped

½ Tbsp lemon juice

1 whole-wheat tortilla or sandwich wrap, warmed

1. In bowl, combine chicken, spinach-artichoke mixture and lemon juice. Roll up in tortilla.

SERVES 1 *About 740 cal, 36 g fat (12 g sat), 52 g pro, 1,330 mg sodium, 55 g carb, 13 g fiber*

Scrambled Egg Toast with Tomato and Parmesan

ACTIVE TIME 10 MIN. | TOTAL TIME 10 MIN.

½ Tbsp olive oil, plus more for drizzling

2 large eggs
Kosher salt and pepper

½ Tbsp chopped fresh chives, plus more for sprinkling

½ Tbsp freshly grated Parmesan

1 slice whole-grain bread, toasted

1 small tomato, sliced

1. Heat oil in a small non-stick skillet on medium-low.

2. In small bowl, whisk together eggs and pinch each salt and pepper.

3. Add eggs to skillet and cook, stirring often, until eggs are beginning to set.

4. Once eggs are nearly set, stir in chives and Parmesan, then spoon over toast. Top with tomato slices and a drizzle of oil if desired. Sprinkle with more chives and pepper.

SERVES 1 *About 345 cal, 19 g fat (5 g sat), 20 g pro, 487 mg sodium, 23 g carb, 4 g fiber*

Sautéed Fish with Tomatoes and Capers

ACTIVE TIME 10 MIN. | TOTAL TIME 20 MIN.

1 Tbsp olive oil

1 small clove garlic, thinly sliced

1 tsp capers, rinsed

1/2 strip lemon zest, thinly sliced

1/4 cup dry rosé or white wine

6 oz Campari tomatoes, quartered

3 pitted kalamata olives, halved
   Kosher salt and pepper

1 6-oz skinless cod fillet
   Chopped parsley, for serving

1. Heat oil, garlic, capers and lemon zest in small skillet on medium, stirring occasionally, until garlic is lightly golden brown, about 2 min.

2. Add wine and simmer 2 min. Stir in tomatoes, olives and 1/4 tsp each salt and pepper. Nestle fish in tomatoes and simmer, covering skillet during last 3 min. of cooking, until cooked and opaque throughout, 6 to 8 min. Sprinkle with parsley, if desired.

SERVES 1 *About 340 cal, 18 g fat (2.5 g sat), 2.5 g pro, 32 mg sodium, 830 g carb, 11 g fiber*

Aleppo Grilled Steak with Farro Salad

ACTIVE TIME 25 MIN. | TOTAL TIME 25 MIN.

1/3 cup quick-cooking farro

1 12-oz strip steak
(about 1½ in. thick)

½ tsp Aleppo pepper
Kosher salt and pepper

2 Tbsp olive oil, divided

4 oz green beans, trimmed
and halved crosswise

½ tsp grated lemon zest
plus 1 Tbsp lemon juice

1 small shallot, thinly sliced

4 pitted Castelvetrano
olives, crushed and
roughly chopped

2 Tbsp flat-leaf parsley,
roughly chopped

2 Tbsp fresh mint, torn
or roughly chopped

1. Heat oven to 425°F. Cook farro per pkg. directions.

2. Heat medium cast-iron skillet on medium-high. Season steak with Aleppo pepper, ¼ tsp salt and ⅛ tsp pepper. Add 1 tsp oil to skillet, then add steak and cook until browned, 3 min. per side.

3. Add green beans to skillet, then transfer skillet to oven and roast steak to desired doneness, 3 to 6 min. for medium. Transfer steak to cutting board and let rest at least 5 min. before slicing. (Save half of steak for lunch tomorrow.) Return green beans to oven until just tender, 2 to 4 min. more.

4. In medium bowl, combine lemon zest and juice, shallots, and ¼ tsp each salt and pepper and let sit 5 min. Stir in remaining 1½ Tbsp oil, then toss with farro. Fold in olives, parsley and mint and serve with steak and green beans.

SERVES 1 (WITH LEFTOVER STEAK) *About 940 cal, 56 g fat (17.5g sat), 49 g pro, 1,210 mg sodium, 59 g carb, 8 g fiber*

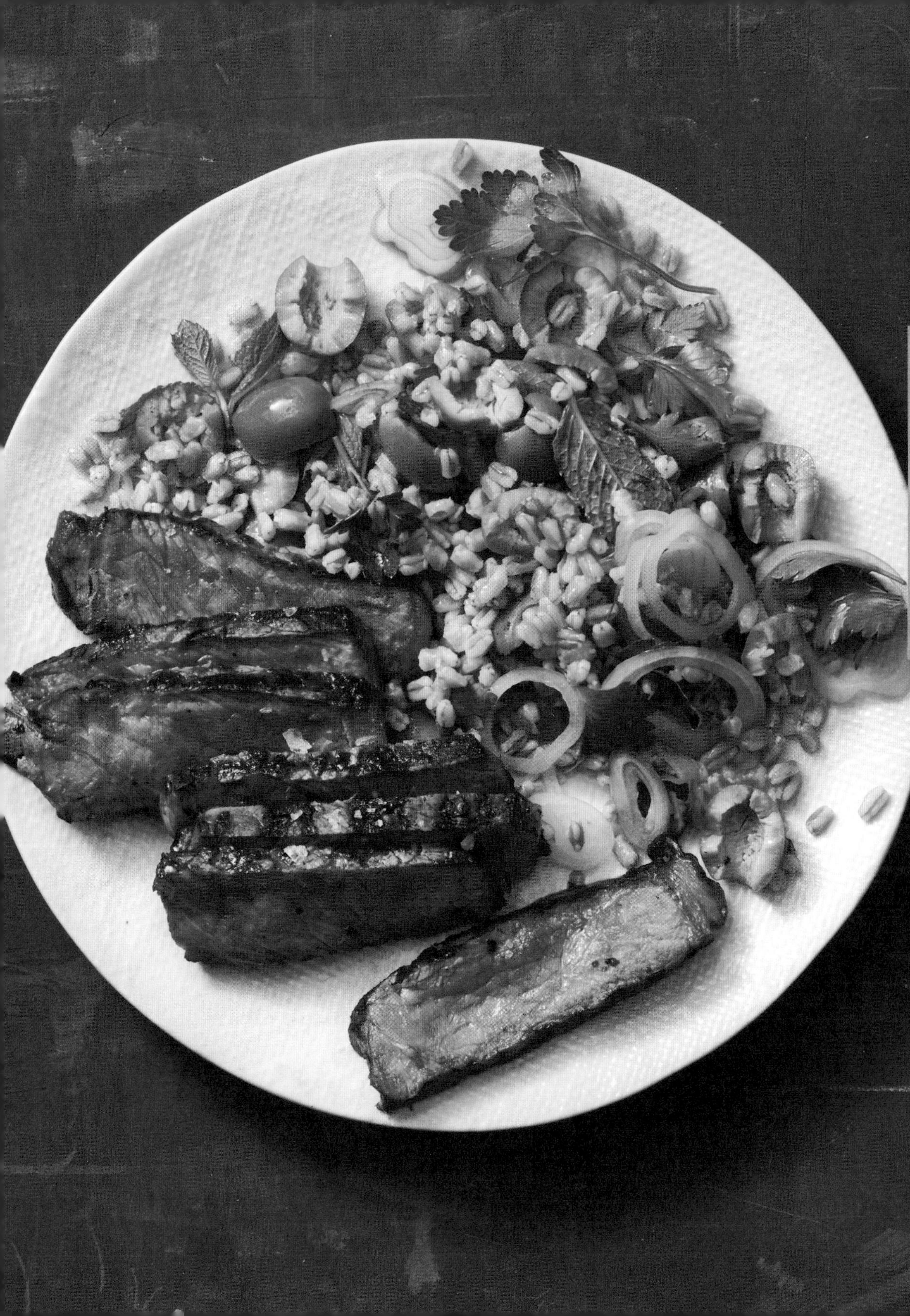

Apricot Pistachio Oatmeal Bowl

ACTIVE TIME 10 MIN. | TOTAL TIME 10 MIN.

¾ cup water
¼ cup quick-cooking
  steel-cut oats
⅛ tsp cinnamon
⅛ tsp cardamom
½ Tbsp tahini
1 tsp honey
1½ Tbsp chopped pistachios
2 dried apricots, chopped

1. In small saucepan, bring water to boil. Add oats, cinnamon and cardamom and cook, stirring occasionally, until tender, 5 to 7 min.

2. In small bowl, combine tahini and honey. Add water to reach a consistency that's easily drizzled.

3. Transfer oats to a bowl, drizzle with tahini mixture and top with pistachios and apricots.

SERVES 1 *About 245 cal, 11 g fat (2 g sat), 7 g pro, 130 mg sodium, 34 g carb, 5 g fiber*

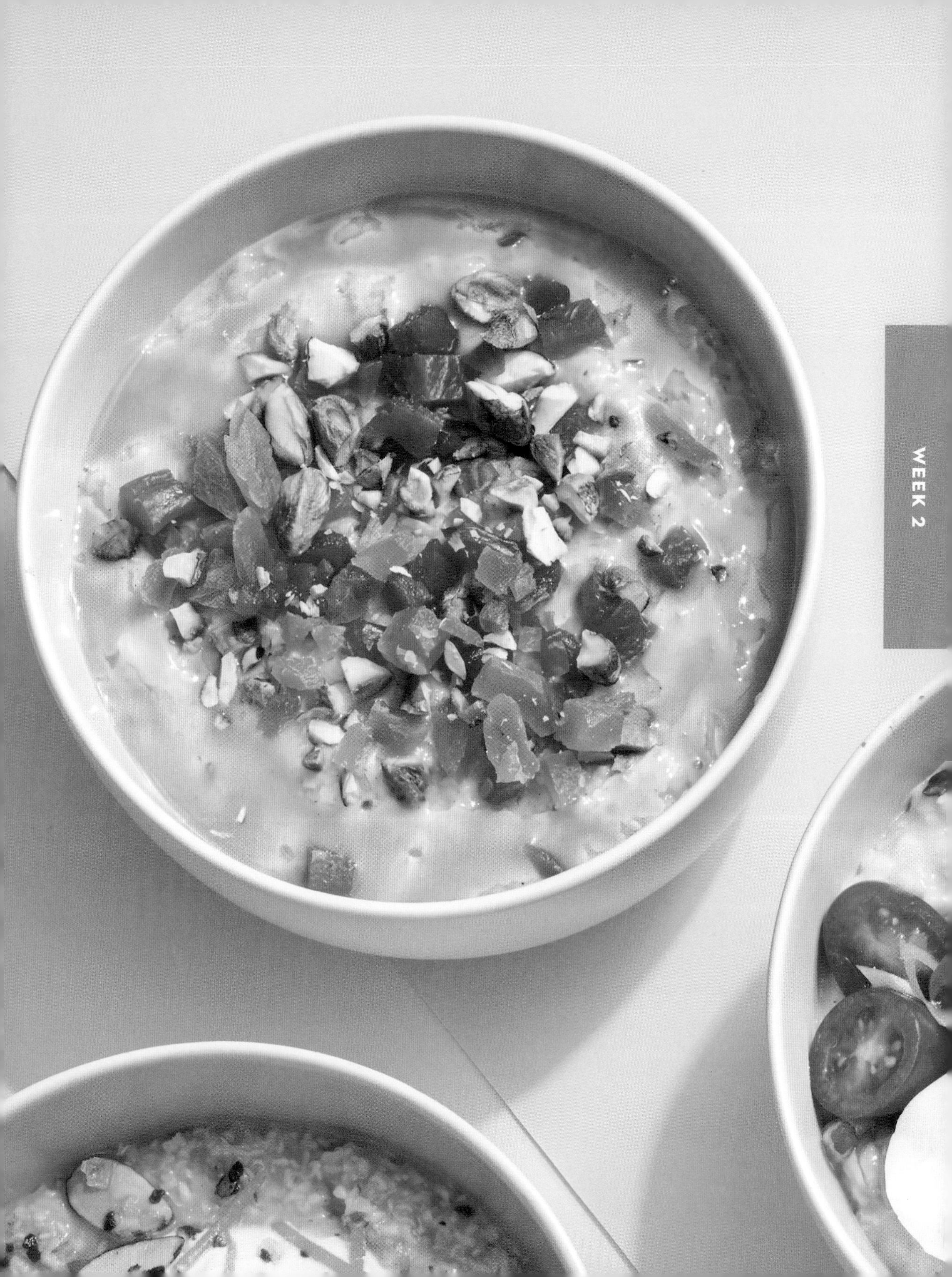

Open-Faced Steak and Arugula Sandwich

ACTIVE TIME 10 MIN. | TOTAL TIME 10 MIN.

¼   small red onion,
      thinly sliced
1   Tbsp lemon juice
      Kosher salt and pepper
1   cup baby arugula
2   tsp olive oil
      Leftover steak from
      Aleppo Grilled Steak with
      Farro Salad (p. 132), sliced
1   slice whole-grain bread,
      toasted
      Shaved Parmesan,
      for serving

1. In small bowl, toss onion with 1 Tbsp lemon juice and pinch each of salt and pepper. Let sit, tossing occasionally, until ready to use.

2. In bowl, toss arugula with oil, 2 tsp lemon juice from onions and pinch each salt and pepper.

3. Arrange steak and arugula on top of bread, then top with marinated onions and Parmesan, if desired.

SERVES 1 *About 605 cal, 36 g fat (11.5 g sat), 46 g pro, 835 mg sodium, 23 g carb, 4 g fiber*

Balsamic Chicken and Onion Salad

ACTIVE TIME 25 MIN. | TOTAL TIME 25 MIN.

2 medium red onions, cut into 1-in.-thick wedges

2½ Tbsp olive oil, divided

2 sprigs fresh thyme, plus more for sprinkling
Kosher salt and pepper

3 Tbsp balsamic vinegar, divided

2 6-oz boneless, skinless chicken breasts

1 head Gem lettuce, leaves separated

½ small bunch arugula, thick stems discarded

½ Tbsp fresh lemon juice

¼ cup flat-leaf parsley leaves

1. Heat oven to 400°F. On large rimmed baking sheet, toss onions with 1½ Tbsp oil, thyme sprigs and ¼ tsp each salt and pepper and roast 10 min.

2. Toss onions with 1 Tbsp vinegar and continue roasting until golden brown and tender, 10 to 15 min. more. Transfer to shallow bowl and sprinkle with additional thyme if desired.

3. Meanwhile, in large skillet on medium, heat 1 Tbsp oil. Season chicken with ½ tsp each salt and pepper and cook until golden brown and cooked through, 7 to 10 min. per side. Remove skillet from heat, add remaining 2 Tbsp vinegar, and turn chicken to coat. Transfer to cutting board, drizzle with any remaining vinegar in pan, and let rest 5 min. before slicing.

4. In large bowl, toss lettuce and arugula with lemon juice, remaining Tbsp oil and ¼ tsp each salt and pepper, then toss with parsley. Transfer 1 chicken breast and ⅓ onions to container for lunch tomorrow. Toss remaining onions into salad and serve with chicken.

SERVES 1 (WITH LEFTOVER CHICKEN AND ONIONS)
About 620 cal, 38.5 g fat (5.5 g sat), 42 g pro, 1,445 mg sodium, 25g carb, 5 g fiber

REINVENTED LEFTOVER: LUNCH

Bulgur with Chicken and Onion

ACTIVE TIME 10 MIN. | TOTAL TIME 10 MIN.

1   cup cooked bulgur
½   Tbsp olive oil
    Kosher salt and pepper
½   cup grape tomatoes, halved
¼   cup flat-leaf parsley,
    roughly chopped
¼   cup fresh mint, roughly chopped
    Leftover onions from Balsamic
    Chicken and Onion Salad (p. 138)
    Leftover chicken from Balsamic
    Chicken and Onion Salad
    (p. 138), sliced

1. In bowl, toss bulgur with oil and pinch each salt and pepper, then fold in tomato, parsley and mint. Serve with onions and chicken.

SERVES 1 *About 615 cal, 25.5 g fat (4 g sat), 47 g pro, 87 mg sodium, 55 g carb, 13 g fiber*

Smoked Salmon Omelet

ACTIVE TIME 10 MIN. | TOTAL TIME 10 MIN.

⅙ small red onion, thinly sliced
½ cup watercress
1 tsp fresh lemon juice
1¼ tsp avocado oil, divided
Kosher salt and pepper
2 large eggs
1 Tbsp nonfat Greek yogurt
1½ oz smoked salmon, torn into pieces

1. In medium bowl, gently toss together red onion, watercress, lemon juice, ¼ tsp oil and pinch each salt and pepper.

2. In nonstick pan, heat remaining 1 tsp oil over medium heat. In separate bowl, whisk 2 eggs and a pinch salt until no visible strands of egg white remain.

3. Add eggs to pan and cook, shaking pan and stirring constantly with silicone spatula, pulling in the more-cooked eggs at the perimeter of the pan to mingle with the less-cooked interior. You should have what looks like wet scrambled eggs about 20 to 25 sec. in.

4. Remove from heat and spread to cover surface of pan, letting residual heat cook and set eggs. Run spatula around pan perimeter and give a shake to loosen omelet.

5. Spread yogurt over bottom half of omelet and top with watercress mixture and smoked salmon. Season with pepper. Fold top half of omelet over filling.

SERVES 1 *About 268 cal, 18 g fat (4.5 g sat), 22 g pro, 681 mg sodium, 3 g carb, 0.5 g fiber*

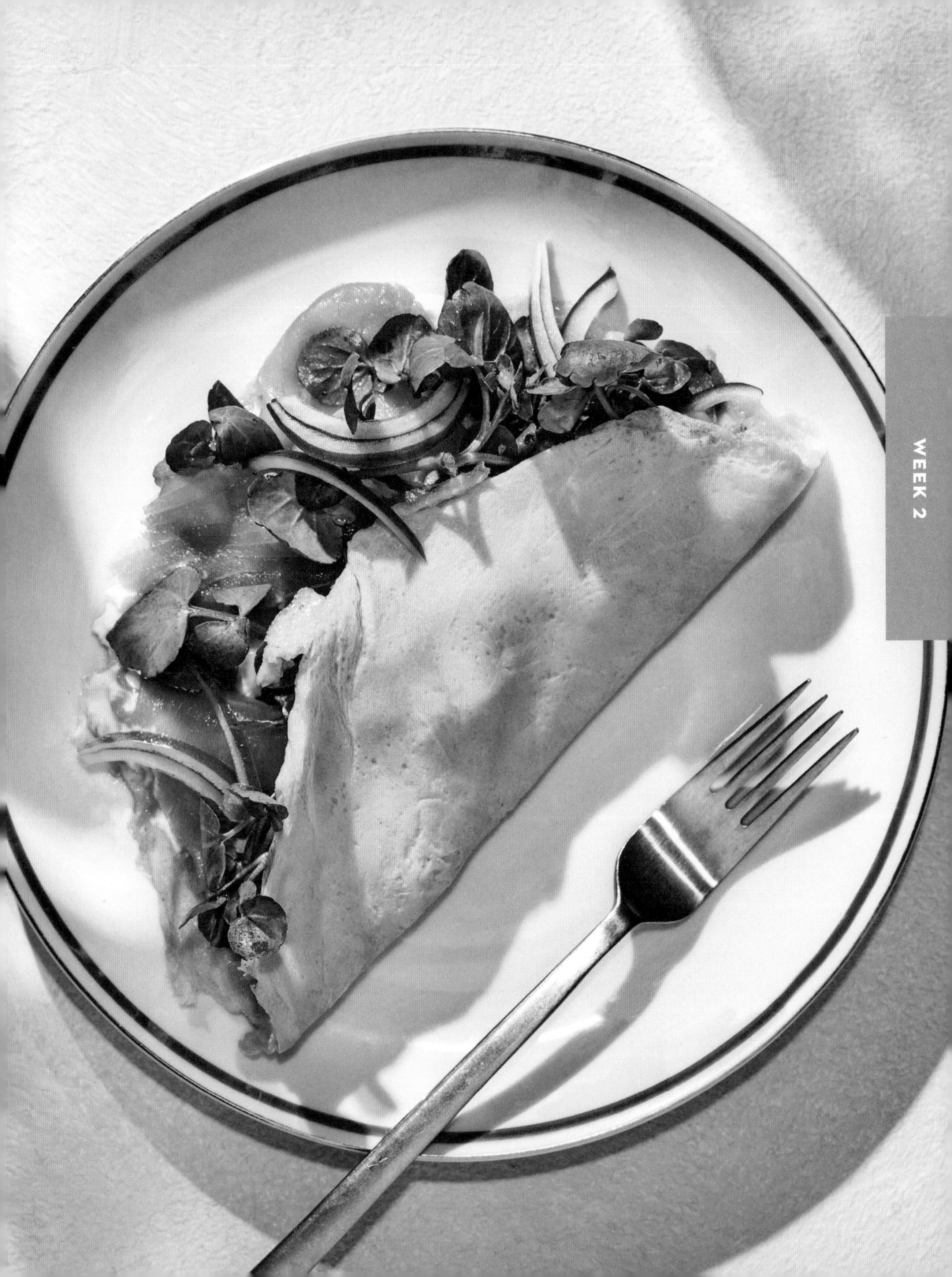

Chickpea Salad Sandwich

ACTIVE TIME 10 MIN. | TOTAL TIME 10 MIN.

1   Tbsp fresh lemon juice
1   Tbsp vegan mayonnaise
½   Tbsp nutritional yeast
      Kosher salt
1   15-oz can low-sodium
      chickpeas, rinsed
1   stalk celery, thinly sliced
½   scallion, sliced
¼   cup parsley, chopped
4   slices whole-grain bread
2   leaves green leaf lettuce
1   Persian cucumber or
      ¼ seedless cucumber,
      peeled into ribbons
½   cup sprouts

1. In large bowl, whisk together lemon juice, mayonnaise, nutritional yeast and pinch salt.

2. Add chickpeas and mash, leaving some larger chunks. Fold in celery, scallion and parsley. Transfer half chickpea mixture to container for another lunch.

3. Assemble 1 sandwich with half each bread, lettuce, chickpea mixture, cucumber and sprouts. Save remaining for another lunch.

SERVES 2 *About 470 cal, 12 g fat (2 g sat fat), 23 g pro, 661 mg sodium, 70 g carb, 16 g fiber*

Lamb Chops and Snap Pea Salad

ACTIVE TIME 25 MIN. | TOTAL TIME 30 MIN.

½ rack lamb, trimmed
(4 to 5 bones total)
2 Tbsp olive oil, divided
1 tsp whole coriander,
crushed
½ tsp ground sumac
Kosher salt and pepper
1½ Tbsp rice vinegar
Pinch sugar
1 small fennel bulb,
very thinly sliced
¼ small red onion,
thinly sliced
6 oz sugar snap peas,
halved lengthwise
4 small radishes, thinly sliced
¼ cup small basil leaves
¼ cup fresh mint leaves
¼ cup flat-leaf parsley leaves

1. Heat oven to 425°F. On rimmed baking sheet, coat lamb with ½ Tbsp oil, then season with coriander, sumac and ¼ tsp each salt and pepper. Roast to desired doneness, 16 to 22 min. for medium-rare. Let rest at least 5 min.

2. Meanwhile, in medium bowl, whisk together remaining 1½ Tbsp oil, vinegar, sugar and ¼ tsp each salt and pepper to dissolve. Add fennel and onion and let sit, tossing occasionally, 10 min., then fold in snap peas, radishes and basil, mint and parsley leaves.

3. Cut 2 chops off lamb and serve with half salad. Refrigerate leftover salad and lamb separately for lunch tomorrow.

SERVES 2 *About 675 cal, 52.5 g fat (18 g sat), 32 g pro, 930 mg sodium, 20 g carb, 8 g fiber*

WEEK 2

AT-A-GLANCE

MENU

DAY 15

BREAKFAST
Spinach-Artichoke
Frittata 🍽

SNACK
1 slice sprouted grain bread

LUNCH
Lamb and Snap Pea
Flatbread ♨

DINNER
Marinated Chicken Salad

DAY 16

BREAKFAST
Mango Passion Fruit Chia
Overnight Shake 🍽

LUNCH
Roasted Butternut Squash
Salad ◍ + 2 servings multi-
grain pita chips (about 18)

DINNER
Air Fryer Salmon and Swiss
Chard + 1 cup cooked quinoa
with 1 Tbsp olive oil, salt and
pepper

DESSERT
100-calorie Greek yogurt ice
cream bar

DAY 17

BREAKFAST
Spinach-Artichoke
Frittata 🍽

SNACK
1 slice sprouted grain bread

LUNCH
Chickpea Salad Sandwich 🍱

SNACK
1 large apple with cinnamon

DINNER
Pork and Scallion Kebabs
with Herbed Couscous

DESSERT
3 pieces dark chocolate

DAY 18

BREAKFAST
2 Buckwheat and Fig Muffins 🍽

LUNCH
Couscous Chicken and
Roasted Squash Tahini
Bowl ♨

SNACK
1 cup lightly salted
pistachios with shells

DINNER
Air Fryer Falafel Salad ◍

DAY 19

BREAKFAST
Spinach Oatmeal Bowl with
Jammy Egg and Tomato Salad

LUNCH
Pork and Scallion Salad ♨

SNACK
1 serving multigrain pita
chips + 3 Tbsp hummus

DINNER
Roasted Shrimp and
Asparagus Pasta

DAY 20

BREAKFAST
Yogurt with Almond
Buckwheat Granola and
Berries ◍

LUNCH
Shrimp and Asparagus
Lettuce Cups ♨

SNACK
1 cup lightly salted
pistachios with shells

DINNER
Chicken and Rice with Feta
Vinaigrette

DAY 21

BREAKFAST
Herbed Egg Bite 🍽 + 2 slices
sprouted grain bread

LUNCH
Chicken Rice Salad ♨

SNACK
1 large apple with cinnamon

DINNER
Smoky Steak and Lentil Salad

DESSERT
100-calorie Greek yogurt ice
cream bar

🍱 Leftover
♨ Reinvented Leftover
🍽 Meal Prepped
◍ Partially Prepped

SHOPPING LIST

Below are exact amounts of everything you will need for Week 3. Be sure to check for leftovers from Week 2 before purchasing items from this list.

PRODUCE

2   large apples
1   lb asparagus
2   cups baby arugula or other baby greens
8   cups baby kale
4   cups baby spinach
1   small banana
2   fresh basil leaves
1/4   cup blueberries
1/2   butternut squash
2   Tbsp fresh cilantro
12   cloves garlic
4   leaves gem lettuce or baby romaine
1   cup grape tomatoes
3   lemons
2   tsp fresh lime juice
2   mini peppers (1 red, 1 orange)
1   ripe mango (about 11 oz total)
1/2   cup fresh mint
3   cups mixed salad greens
1/2   cup flat-leaf parsley
2   Persian cucumbers
13   scallions
1   small head radicchio
2 1/2   small red onions
1/2   small bunch red Swiss chard

MEAT & SEAFOOD

1   8- to 9-oz boneless, skinless chicken breast
2   6-oz boneless, skinless chicken breasts
1/2   lb pork tenderloin
1   5-oz fillet salmon
1/2   lb large peeled and deveined shrimp
1   1-in. strip steak (about 12 oz total)

REFRIGERATED & DAIRY

1/2   cup cashew milk (or milk of choice) plus more for serving
11   eggs
1   oz feta
3   Tbsp hummus
3/4   cup nonfat Greek yogurt

FROZEN

1   12-oz pkg. frozen quartered artichoke hearts
2   100-calorie Greek yogurt ice cream bar
1/3   cup frozen passion fruit pulp (we used Pitaya brand)

BREAD & BAKERY

4   slices sprouted grain bread
1   piece whole-wheat flatbread or pita

PANTRY

1/4   tsp agave or honey
1   Tbsp sliced almonds
1/2   cup basmati rice
1/2   Tbsp chia seeds
2   15-oz cans chickpeas
1/2   Tbsp finely shredded unsweetened coconut, toasted
1   tsp ground coriander
3/4   cup couscous
1/3   cup crispy chickpea snacks
1   tsp ground cumin
3   pieces dark chocolate
1   Tbsp dried cranberries
1   15-oz can lentils
3   servings multigrain pita chips
2/3   cup Parmesan, plus more for serving
2   cups lightly salted pistachios with shells
1/3   cup quinoa
1/4   cup quick-cooking steel-cut oats
1/2   Tbsp smoked paprika, plus more for serving
1/8   tsp ground sumac
1/4   cup tahini
1   Tbsp toasted walnuts
3   oz whole-wheat spaghetti

SUNDAY PREP

WEEK 3

½ BUTTERNUT SQUASH
(½ cut into half moons and
½ cut into 1-in. pieces; roast or
air-fry) for Roasted Butternut
Squash Salad (p. 162) and
Couscous Chicken and Roasted
Squash Tahini Bowl (p. 168)

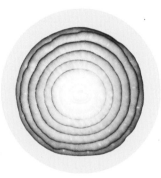

1 SMALL RED ONION
(roast or air-fry) for
Roasted Butternut
Squash Salad (p. 162)

TAHINI DRESSING
for Roasted Butternut Squash
Salad (p. 162)

FALAFEL (P. 66)
for Air Fryer Falafel Salad
(p. 170)

1 JAMMY EGG (P. 42)
for Spinach Oatmeal Bowl
with Jammy Egg
and Tomato Salad (p. 172)

**MANGO PASSION FRUIT CHIA
OVERNIGHT SHAKE (P. 54)**

MEAL PLAN: Week 3

DAY 15

BREAKFAST
Spinach-Artichoke
Frittata 🔲 (p. 52)

SNACK
1 slice sprouted grain bread

LUNCH
Lamb and Snap Pea
Flatbread ♨ (p. 158)

DINNER
Marinated Chicken
Salad (p. 160)
Refrigerate remaining
chicken in airtight container
for Day 18 lunch.

NOTES TO SELF

WATER

MOVEMENT Y ☐ N ☐

ACTIVITY	DURATION	INTENSITY

SLEEP
Bedtime Last Night: _____ : _____
Wake Time This Morning: _____ : _____

MOOD

CONNECTION

MEAL PLAN: Week 3

DAY 16

BREAKFAST
Mango Passion Fruit Chia
Overnight Shake ▢▯ (p. 54)

LUNCH
Roasted Butternut Squash
Salad ◍ (p. 162)
+ 2 servings multigrain
pita chips (about 18)

DINNER
Air Fryer Salmon and
Swiss Chard (p. 164)
+ 1 cup cooked quinoa with
1 Tbsp olive oil, salt and
pepper

DESSERT
100-calorie Greek yogurt
ice cream bar

NOTES TO SELF

WATER

MOVEMENT Y ☐ N ☐

ACTIVITY	DURATION	INTENSITY

SLEEP

Bedtime Last Night: _____ : _____

Wake Time This Morning: _____ : _____

MOOD

CONNECTION

DAY 17

BREAKFAST
Spinach-Artichoke
Frittata 🍽 (p. 52)

SNACK
1 slice sprouted grain bread

LUNCH
Chickpea Salad Sandwich 🍱
(p. 142)

SNACK
1 large apple with cinnamon

DINNER
Pork and Scallion
Kebabs with Herbed
Couscous (p. 166)

DESSERT
3 pieces dark chocolate

NOTES TO SELF

WATER

MOVEMENT Y☐ N☐

ACTIVITY	DURATION	INTENSITY

SLEEP
Bedtime Last Night: _____ : _____
Wake Time This Morning: _____ : _____

MOOD

CONNECTION

MEAL PLAN: Week 3

DAY 18

BREAKFAST
2 Buckwheat and
Fig Muffins 🍽 (p. 50)

LUNCH
Couscous Chicken and
Roasted Squash Tahini
Bowl ♨ (p. 168)

SNACK
1 cup lightly salted
pistachios with shells

DINNER
Air Fryer Falafel
Salad ◍ (p. 170)

WATER

MOVEMENT Y ☐ N ☐

ACTIVITY	DURATION	INTENSITY

SLEEP
Bedtime Last Night: _____ : _____
Wake Time This Morning: _____ : _____

NOTES TO SELF

MOOD

CONNECTION

DAY 19

BREAKFAST

Spinach Oatmeal Bowl with Jammy Egg and Tomato Salad (p. 172)

LUNCH

Pork and Scallion Salad ♨ (p. 174)

SNACK

1 serving multigrain pita chips + 3 Tbsp hummus

DINNER

Roasted Shrimp and Asparagus Pasta (p. 176) Refrigerate remaining vegetables and shrimp in airtight container for Day 20 lunch.

NOTES TO SELF

WATER

MOVEMENT Y☐ N☐

ACTIVITY	DURATION	INTENSITY

SLEEP

Bedtime Last Night: _____ : _____

Wake Time This Morning: _____ : _____

MOOD

CONNECTION

MEAL PLAN: Week 3

DAY 20

BREAKFAST
Yogurt with Almond
Buckwheat Granola and
Berries ⬤ (p. 172)

LUNCH
Shrimp and Asparagus
Lettuce Cups ♨ (p. 177)

SNACK
1 cup lightly salted
pistachios with shells

DINNER
Chicken and Rice with Feta
Vinaigrette (p. 178)
Refrigerate remaining in
airtight container for
Day 21 lunch.

NOTES TO SELF

WATER

MOVEMENT Y☐ N☐

ACTIVITY	DURATION	INTENSITY

SLEEP

Bedtime Last Night: _____ : _____

Wake Time This Morning: _____ : _____

MOOD

CONNECTION

DAY 21

BREAKFAST
Herbed Egg Bite 🍳
(p. 40) + 2 slices sprouted
grain bread

LUNCH
Chicken Rice
Salad 🥗 (p. 180)

SNACK
1 large apple with
cinnamon

DINNER
Smoky Steak and
Lentil Salad (p. 182)
Refrigerate remaining in
airtight container for
Day 22 lunch.

DESSERT
100-calorie Greek yogurt
ice cream bar

NOTES TO SELF

WATER

MOVEMENT Y ☐ N ☐

ACTIVITY	DURATION	INTENSITY

SLEEP
Bedtime Last Night: _____ : _____
Wake Time This Morning: _____ : _____

MOOD

CONNECTION

WEEK 3
RECIPES

Lamb and Snap Pea Flatbread

ACTIVE TIME 10 MIN. | TOTAL TIME 10 MIN.

2   Tbsp nonfat Greek yogurt
1/8 tsp ground sumac
     Kosher salt and pepper
1   piece whole-wheat flat-
     bread or pita, warmed
     Leftover Lamb Chops and
     Snap Pea Salad (p. 144)

1. In bowl, combine yogurt, sumac and pinch each salt and pepper; spread onto flatbread.

2. Slice leftover lamb and arrange on yogurt, top with pea salad and spoon leftover dressing over top.

SERVES 1 *About 900 cal, 54.5 g fat (19 g sat), 45 g pro, 1,575 mg sodium, 59 g carb, 12 g fiber*

WEEK 3

Marinated Chicken Salad

ACTIVE TIME 25 MIN. | TOTAL TIME 40 MIN. PLUS MARINATING & RESTING

2 tsp white wine vinegar
½ Tbsp red wine vinegar
½ small clove garlic
½ tsp Dijon mustard
¼ tsp agave or honey
2 fresh basil leaves
   Kosher salt and pepper
2½ Tbsp olive oil
   Pinch red pepper flakes
   Pinch dried oregano
2 6-oz boneless, skinless
   chicken breasts
2 mini peppers (1 red,
   1 orange), thinly sliced
¼ cup grape tomatoes,
   halved
⅛ small red onion,
   thinly sliced
3 cups mixed salad greens,
   torn into bite-size pieces
   Shaved Parmesan,
   for serving

1. In mini blender, combine vinegars, garlic, mustard, agave, basil and ½ tsp each salt and pepper; blend until smooth. Add oil and blend on low until just incorporated but not emulsified, about 10 sec. Stir in red pepper flakes and oregano.

2. In bowl, coat chicken with 2 Tbsp dressing and marinate at least 10 min. at room temp or up to overnight in refrigerator.

3. Meanwhile, transfer 1 Tbsp remaining dressing to large bowl. Add peppers, tomatoes and onion and toss to coat.

4. Heat air fryer to 400°F. Add chicken and cook 4 min. Using tongs, flip and cook until golden brown and cooked through, 8 to 9 min. Transfer to cutting board and let rest 5 min. before slicing (only slice the piece you're eating for dinner tonight; refrigerate remaining chicken for lunch another day).

5. Add greens to peppers and toss to coat. Top with Parmesan, if desired, and serve with sliced chicken and any remaining dressing, if desired.

SERVES 1 (WITH LEFTOVER CHICKEN) *About 400 cal, 21 g fat (3.5 g sat), 38 g pro, 620 mg sodium, 16 g carb, 5 g fiber*

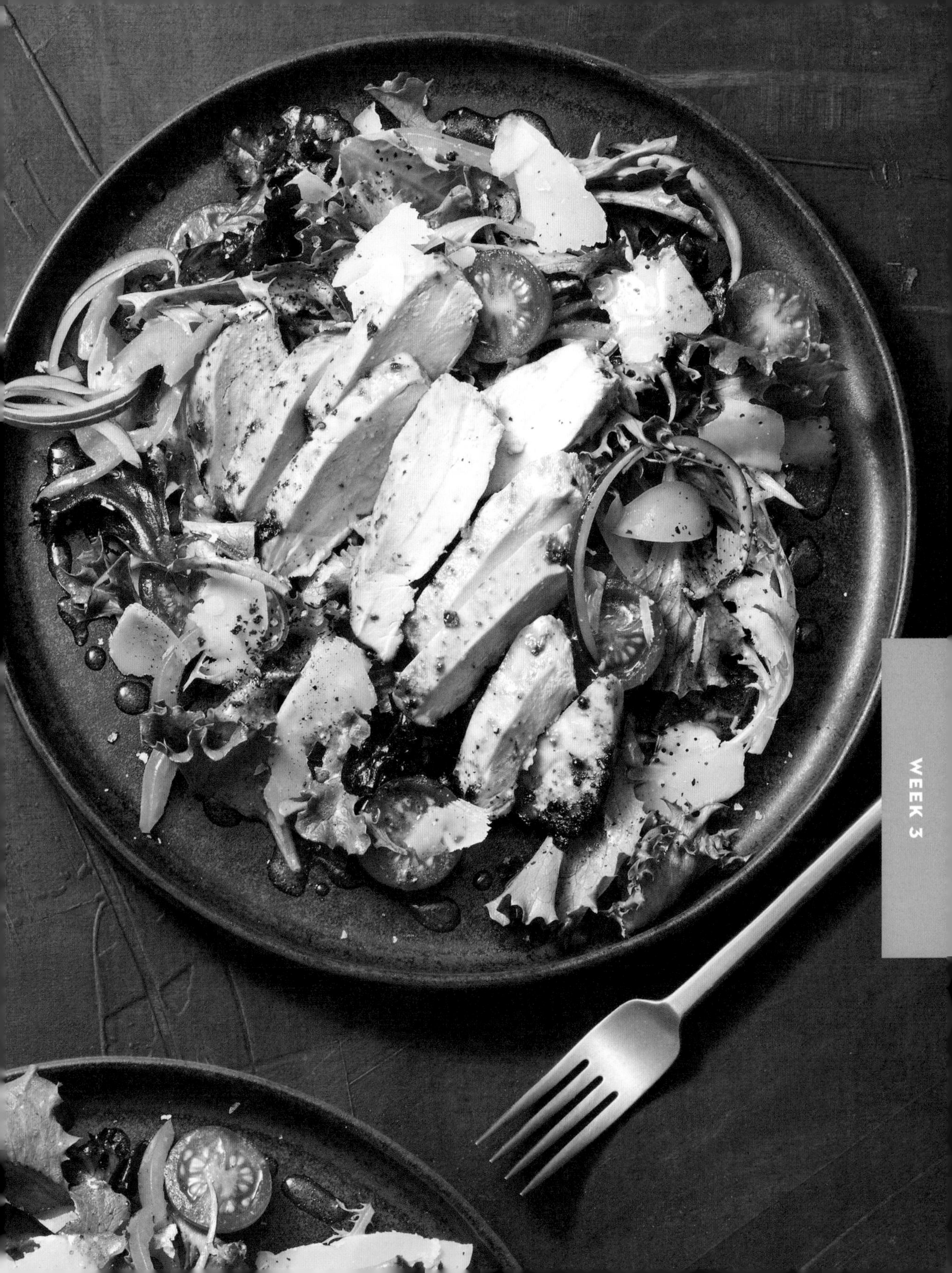

Roasted Butternut Squash Salad

ACTIVE TIME 15 MIN. | TOTAL TIME 15 MIN.

4 oz roasted butternut squash
1 small red onion, roasted
2 cups baby kale
2 Tbsp Tahini Dressing (recipe below)
½ tsp lemon zest
2 Tbsp fresh cilantro, chopped
1 Tbsp sliced almonds, toasted

1. Reheat roasted squash and red onion, if desired, then toss with kale. Transfer vegetables to a serving bowl or plate, drizzle with dressing and sprinkle with lemon zest, cilantro and almonds.

SERVES 1 *About 215 cal, 11.5 g fat (2 g sat), 8 g pro, 180 mg sodium, 26 g carb, 9 g fiber*

TAHINI DRESSING
Whisk together ¼ cup **tahini**, 2 Tbsp **lemon juice**, 2 Tbsp **water** and ¼ tsp **salt**, adding more water if dressing is too thick.
SERVES 6 *Per 1 Tbsp about 45 cal, 4 g fat (0.5 g sat), 1 g pro, 70 mg sodium, 2 g carb, 1 g fiber*

WEEK 3

Air Fryer Salmon and Swiss Chard

ACTIVE TIME 25 MIN. | TOTAL TIME 25 MIN.

1   small red onion,
    sliced ½ in. thick
1   Tbsp olive oil, divided
    Kosher salt and pepper
½   small bunch red Swiss
    chard, thick stems dis-
    carded, leaves chopped
1   clove garlic, sliced
1   5-oz salmon fillet

1. Heat air fryer to 385°F. Toss onion with ½ Tbsp oil and a pinch each of kosher salt and pepper and air-fry 5 min.

2. Toss with red Swiss chard, garlic, ½ Tbsp oil and pinch each of salt and pepper and air-fry until chard and onion are just tender, about 5 min. more. Transfer to plate.

3. Season salmon with pinch each salt and pepper and air-fry at 400°F until skin is crispy and salmon is opaque throughout, 8 to 10 min.

SERVES 1 *About 350 cal, 19 g fat (3 g sat), 32 g pro, 730 mg sodium, 13 g carb, 4 g fiber*

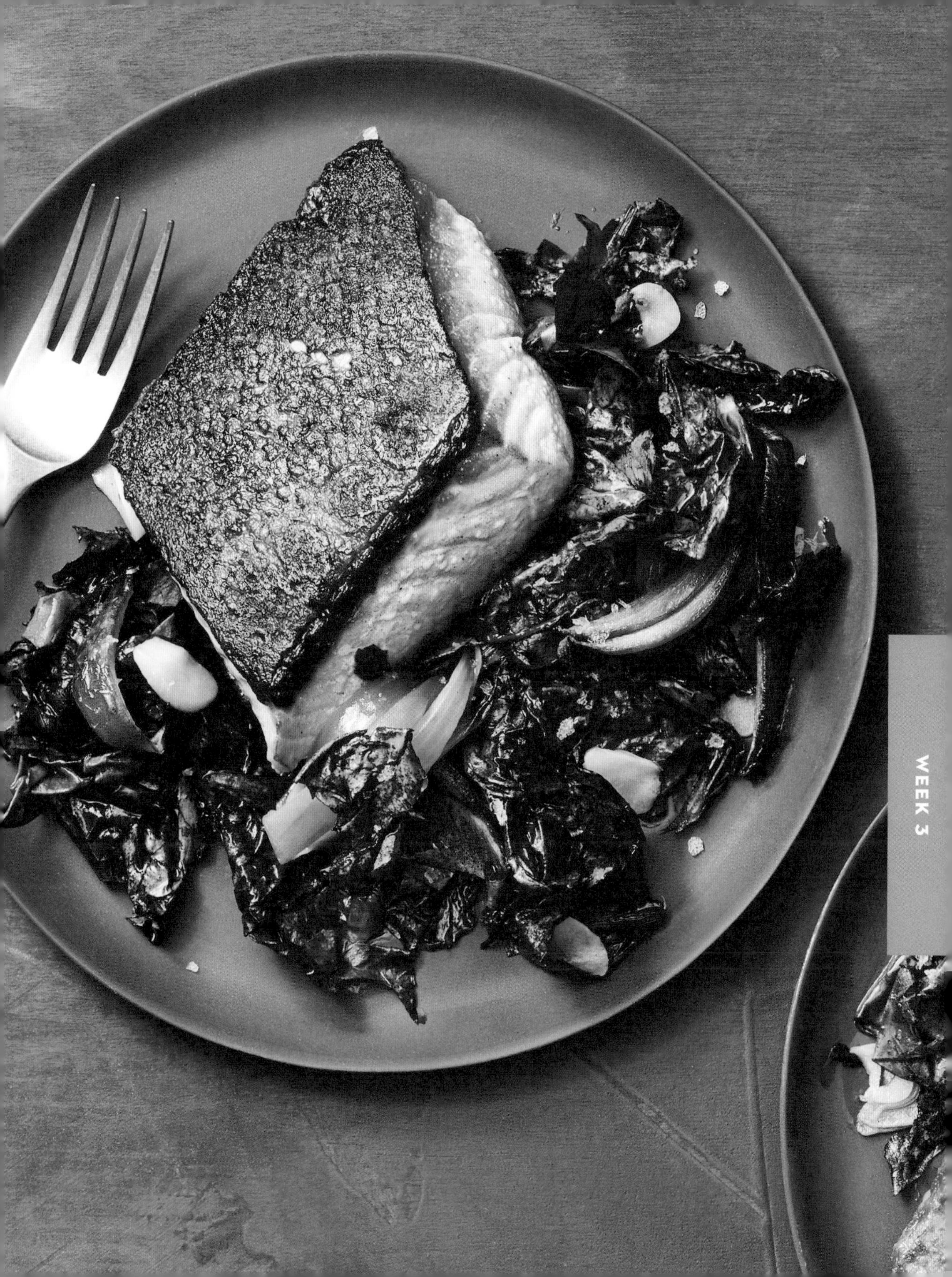

Pork and Scallion Kebabs with Herbed Couscous

ACTIVE TIME 25 MIN. | TOTAL TIME 25 MIN.

1   lemon
1   clove garlic, pressed or finely grated
1   Tbsp olive oil
     Kosher salt and pepper
½   lb pork tenderloin
2   scallions, each cut into 4 2-in. pieces
½   cup couscous
¼   cup fresh mint leaves, finely chopped
¼   cup fresh flat-leaf parsley, finely chopped
1   Persian cucumber, cut into very small pieces
½   oz feta cheese, crumbled
     Skewers

1. Heat grill or grill pan to medium high. In medium bowl, finely grate zest of lemon; transfer half to second bowl. To one bowl, squeeze in 1 Tbsp juice. Add garlic, oil and ⅛ tsp each salt and pepper and mix to combine. Thinly slice the pork on a diagonal, add to bowl along with scallions and toss to coat.

2. To second bowl, add couscous and mix to combine. Add ½ cup plus 2 Tbsp boiling water, cover and let sit until all water has been absorbed, about 10 min.

3. Meanwhile, thread pork and scallions onto skewers and grill until just cooked through, 2 to 3 min. per side. Squeeze remaining lemon juice over top; transfer half to plate and transfer remaining to container for lunch another day.

4. Fluff couscous and transfer half to container for lunch tomorrow. Toss remaining couscous with mint, parsley, cucumber and feta. Serve herbed couscous with pork.

SERVES 1 *About 460 cal, 17 g fat (5.5 g sat), 34 g pro, 325 mg sodium, 42 g carb, 5 g fiber*

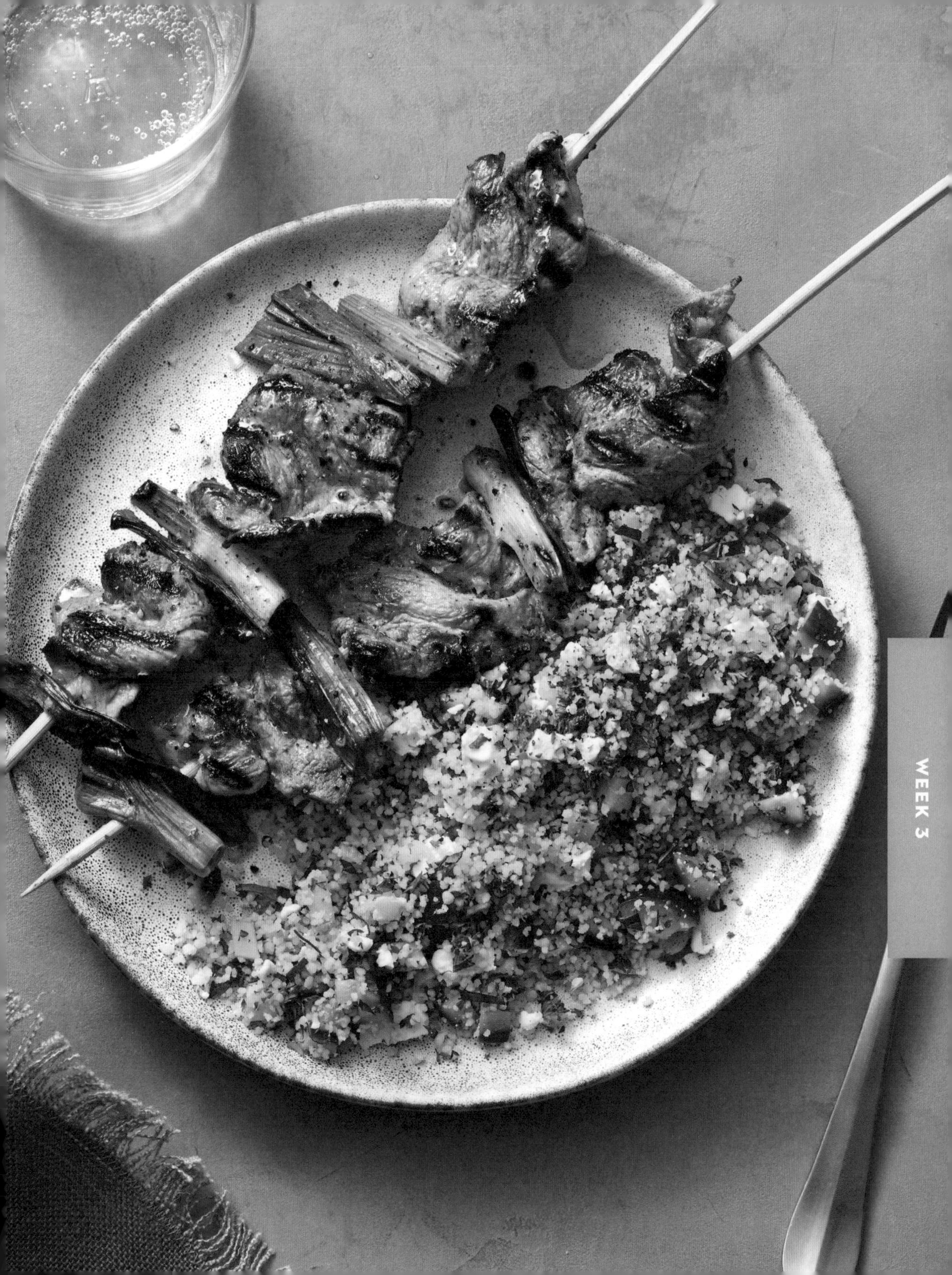

Couscous Chicken and Roasted Squash Tahini Bowl

ACTIVE TIME 10 MIN. | TOTAL TIME 10 MIN.

Leftover couscous from Pork and Scallion Kebabs with Herbed Couscous (p. 166)

4 oz roasted butternut squash (pieces)

1½ cups baby kale

Leftover chicken from Marinated Chicken Salad (p. 160), sliced

1 Tbsp dried cranberries

1 Tbsp toasted walnuts

2 Tbsp Tahini Dressing from Roasted Butternut Squash Salad (p. 162)

1. In bowl, place couscous, squash, kale and chicken. Sprinkle with cranberries and walnuts and drizzle with Tahini Dressing.

SERVES 1 *About 650 cal, 26 g fat (4 g sat), 46 g pro, 510 mg sodium, 61 g carb, 10 g fiber*

Air Fryer Falafel Salad

ACTIVE TIME 15 MIN. | TOTAL TIME 15 MIN.

6   balls frozen Falafel (p. 66)
½   Tbsp olive oil
2   tsp lemon juice
     Kosher salt and pepper
1   Persian cucumber, thinly
     sliced on bias
1   small scallion, whites finely
     chopped; greens thinly
     sliced
2   cups baby kale
2   Tbsp fresh parsley leaves
1   Tbsp fresh mint leaves
     Greek yogurt, for topping

1. Heat air fryer to 375°F. Cook falafel until heated through, 10 to 12 min.

2. Meanwhile, in large bowl, whisk together oil, lemon juice and pinch each salt and pepper. Toss with cucumber and scallion whites and let sit 5 min.

3. Add kale, parsley, mint and scallion greens and toss to combine. Serve with falafel and dollop of yogurt, if desired.

SERVES 1 *About 330 cal, 14 g fat (2 g sat), 13 g pro, 680 mg sodium, 40 g carb, 12 g fiber*

WEEK 3

Spinach Oatmeal Bowl with Jammy Egg and Tomato Salad

ACTIVE TIME 10 MIN. | TOTAL TIME 10 MIN.

¼ cup quick-cooking
steel-cut oats
Kosher salt
¼ cup grape tomatoes,
sliced in half
2 tsp olive oil
1 scallion, thinly sliced
¾ cup baby spinach
1 Jammy Egg (p. 42), halved

1. In small saucepan, bring ¾ cup water to boil. Add oats and pinch of salt and cook, stirring occasionally, until tender, 5 to 7 min.

2. Meanwhile, in bowl, toss tomatoes, oil, scallion and pinch salt.

3. Remove oatmeal from heat and fold in spinach to wilt. Transfer to bowl and top with tomatoes and jammy egg.

SERVES 1 *About 256 cal, 15.5 g fat (3 g sat), 11 g pro, 344 mg sodium, 22 g carb, 3 g fiber*

Yogurt with Almond Buckwheat Granola and Berries

ACTIVE TIME 5 MIN. | TOTAL TIME 5 MIN.

½ cup nonfat Greek yogurt
¼ cup Almond Buckwheat
Granola (p. 44)
1 small banana, sliced
¼ cup blueberries
Pure maple syrup,
for drizzling

1. Spoon yogurt into bowl, top with granola, banana and berries and drizzle with maple syrup, if desired.

SERVES 1 *About 320 cal, 10 g fat (1 g sat), 17 g pro, 235 mg sodium, 45 g carb, 6 g fiber*

WEEK 3

Pork and Scallion Salad

ACTIVE TIME 10 MIN. | TOTAL TIME 10 MIN.

2   tsp fresh lime juice
¼   tsp honey
     Kosher salt and pepper
⅛   small red onion,
     thinly sliced
½   Tbsp olive oil
2   cups baby arugula or
     other baby greens
     Leftover grilled pork and
     scallions from Pork and
     Scallion Kebabs with
     Herbed Couscous (p. 166)
⅓   cup crispy chickpeas

1. In bowl, whisk together lime juice, honey and pinch salt and pepper; toss with onion; let sit, tossing occasionally, 5 min.

2. Whisk in olive oil, then toss with arugula, then leftover pork and scallions and crispy chickpeas.

SERVES 1 *About 415 cal, 25 g fat (5 g sat), 30 g pro, 460 mg sodium, 20 g carb, 5 g fiber*

WEEK 3

Roasted Shrimp and Asparagus Pasta

ACTIVE TIME 20 MIN. | TOTAL TIME 20 MIN.

3   oz whole-wheat spaghetti
1   lb asparagus, trimmed and
     cut into thirds
2   cloves garlic, chopped
1½   Tbsp olive oil, divided
     Kosher salt and pepper
1   lemon
½   lb large peeled and
     deveined shrimp
¼   tsp red pepper flakes, plus
     more for serving
1-2 Tbsp flat-leaf parsley,
     chopped
     Grated Parmesan,
     for serving

1. Heat oven to 425°F. In a large pot, cook pasta per pkg. directions. Reserve ½ cup pasta cooking water; drain pasta and return to pot.

2. On rimmed baking sheet, toss asparagus and garlic with 1 Tbsp oil and ¼ tsp each salt and pepper. Zest lemon and set zest aside. Halve lemon and place on baking sheet, cut sides down; roast 4 min.

3. Meanwhile, toss shrimp with remaining ½ Tbsp oil, then red pepper flakes, ¼ tsp salt and ⅛ tsp pepper. Nestle shrimp on tray with asparagus and continue roasting until shrimp are opaque throughout and asparagus is just tender, 5 to 7 min. more.

4. Transfer lemon halves to plate, then transfer half the vegetables and half the shrimp to airtight container for lunch tomorrow. Transfer remaining vegetables, shrimp and any pan juices to pot with pasta.

5. Squeeze 1 Tbsp roasted lemon juice over top and toss to combine, adding some reserved pasta water if pasta seems dry. Toss with parsley and serve sprinkled with ¼ tsp reserved lemon zest, grated Parmesan and additional red pepper flakes if desired. Refrigerate remaining roasted lemons and zest along with vegetables for lunch tomorrow.

SERVES 1 (WITH LEFTOVER VEGETABLES AND SHRIMP)
About 570 cal, 15 g fat (2 g sat), 40 g pro, 645 mg sodium, 79 g carb, 12 g fiber

REINVENTED LEFTOVER: LUNCH

Shrimp and Asparagus Lettuce Cups

ACTIVE TIME 10 MIN. | TOTAL TIME 10 MIN.

¼ cup couscous
Leftover shrimp, asparagus
and roasted lemon from
Roasted Shrimp and
Asparagus Pasta (p. 176)

1 scallion (dark green only),
thinly sliced

4 small leaves mint, chopped
plus more for serving

4 leaves gem lettuce
or baby romaine

1. In small bowl, place couscous and squeeze 1 Tbsp roasted lemon juice on top, then add ⅓ cup boiling water. Cover and let sit 5 min.

2. Meanwhile, roughly chop leftover shrimp and asparagus. Fluff couscous with fork, fold in scallion and ¼ tsp leftover lemon zest, then fold in mint.

3. Serve couscous in lettuce leaves, top with shrimp and asparagus and additional mint, if desired.

SERVES 1 *About 425 cal, 15 g fat (2 g sat), 32 g pro, 656 mg sodium, 44 g carb, 6 g fiber*

Chicken and Rice with Feta Vinaigrette

ACTIVE TIME 20 MIN. | TOTAL TIME 30 MIN.

1   lemon, plus lemon
    wedges for serving
3   garlic cloves, smashed
½   cup basmati rice, rinsed
    Kosher salt and pepper
1   8- to 9-oz boneless,
    skinless chicken breast
¼   tsp honey
1   small scallion,
    finely chopped
2   Tbsp olive oil
2   Tbsp fresh mint, chopped
1   cup baby spinach
½   oz feta, cut into chunks

1. Heat oven to 375°F. Using vegetable peeler, remove 2 strips lemon zest and add to small saucepan along with garlic, rice and ¼ tsp salt. Add ½ cup plus 2 Tbsp water and stir to combine. Bring to boil, reduce heat to simmer, cover and cook until just tender and water is absorbed, 15 min. Remove from heat, let stand 3 min.

2. Place chicken on small baking sheet. Season with ¼ tsp salt and ⅛ tsp pepper and bake until cooked through, 18 to 20 min. Let rest 3 min.

3. Meanwhile, prepare dressing. Squeeze 2 tsp lemon juice into bowl and whisk in honey and pinch each salt and pepper to dissolve. Stir in scallion, oil, then mint.

4. Discard lemon zest and fluff rice. Transfer ½ cup to container for lunch tomorrow. Add spinach to saucepan, cover and let sit for 5 min., then fold into rice.

5. Slice half chicken and serve over rice, spooning half mint dressing on top. Serve with half feta and lemon wedges if desired. Refrigerate remaining dressing and chicken along with rice and remaining feta for lunch tomorrow.

SERVES 2 *About 440 cal, 18.5 g fat (4 g sat), 30 g pro, 665 mg sodium, 37 g carb, 2 g fiber*

Chicken Rice Salad

ACTIVE TIME 10 MIN. | TOTAL TIME 10 MIN.

½ cup leftover cooked rice from Chicken and Rice with Feta Vinaigrette (p. 178)

1½ cups baby spinach, roughly chopped
Leftover cooked chicken breast from Chicken and Rice with Feta Vinaigrette (p. 178), shredded

½ cup grape tomatoes, sliced
Leftover mint dressing from Chicken and Rice with Feta Vinaigrette (p. 178)

1. In microwave, reheat rice until just warm. Fold in spinach, chicken, tomatoes, then dressing.

SERVES 1 *About 500 cal, 18.5 g fat (4 g sat), 34 g pro, 805 mg sodium, 52 g carb, 6 g fiber*

WEEK 3

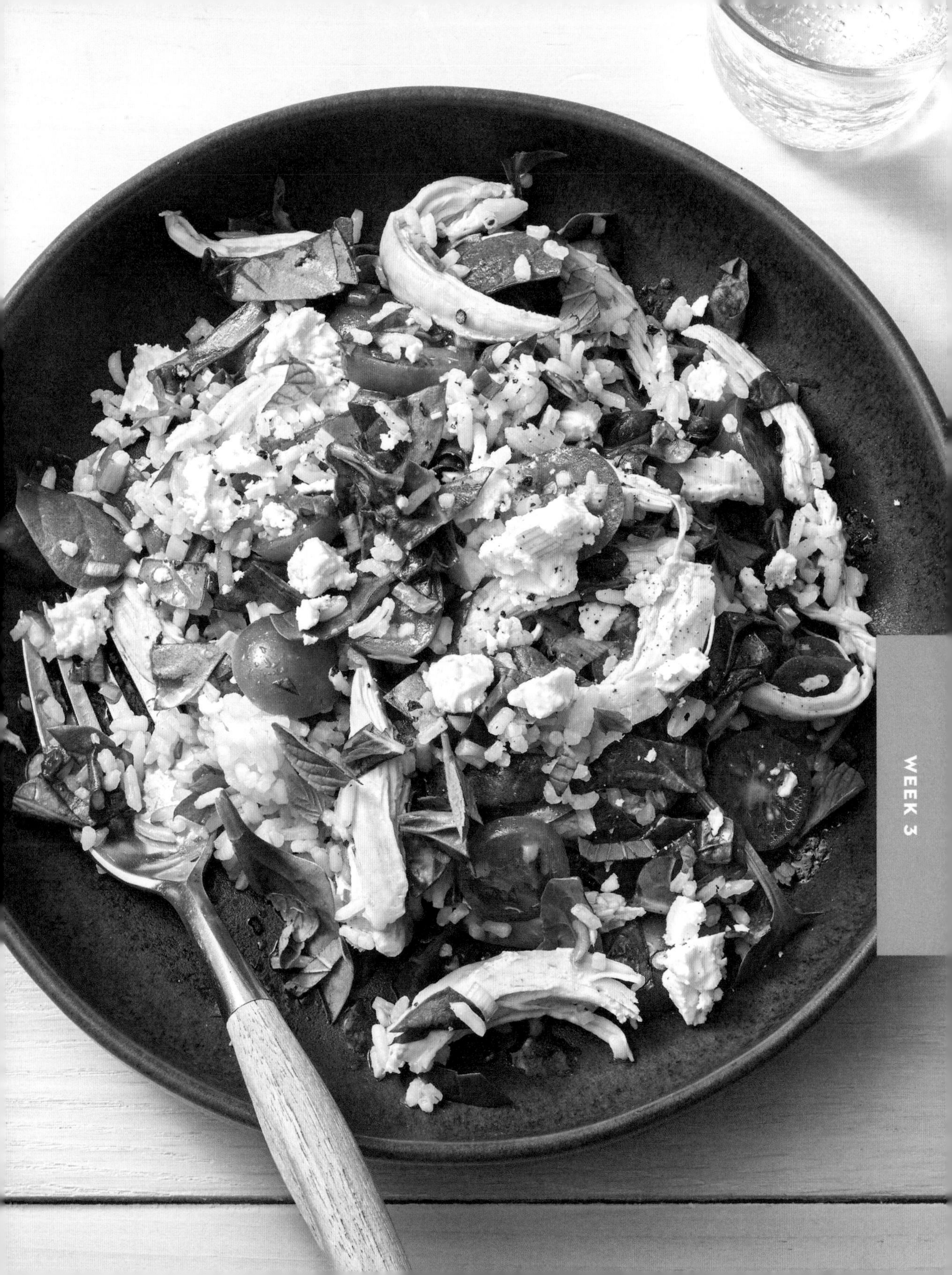

Smoky Steak and Lentil Salad

ACTIVE TIME 30 MIN. | TOTAL TIME 30 MIN.

½ Tbsp lemon juice

½ tsp Dijon mustard
   Kosher salt and pepper

¼ small red onion,
   finely chopped

1 1-in. strip steak (about
   12 oz total), trimmed

½ Tbsp smoked paprika, plus
   more for serving

1 Tbsp olive oil, divided

1 15-oz can lentils, rinsed
   and drained

1 small head radicchio,
   chopped

2 cups baby kale

1. In large bowl, whisk together lemon juice, mustard and ¼ tsp each salt and pepper; stir in onion and let sit 5 min.

2. Meanwhile, pat steak dry with paper towels, then rub with paprika and ½ tsp each salt and pepper; shake off any excess.

3. In large skillet on medium, heat ½ Tbsp oil and cook steak to desired doneness, 4 to 5 min. per side for medium-rare. Transfer to a cutting board and let rest at least 5 min. before slicing half for dinner tonight.

4. Add lentils to onion and toss to combine. Toss with remaining ½ Tbsp oil and ¼ tsp each salt and pepper. Transfer half to container for lunch tomorrow, then toss remaining lentils and onion with half each radicchio and kale. Serve with half of the sliced steak. Refrigerate lentils, remaining half each radicchio and kale, and steak separately for lunch tomorrow.

SERVES 2 *About 600 cal, 28.5 g fat (9.5 g sat), 52 g pro, 1,245 mg sodium, 33 g carb, 17 g fiber*

AT-A-GLANCE

MENU

DAY 22

BREAKFAST
Banana Chocolate Chip Muffin ▭

LUNCH
Smoky Steak and Lentil Salad ▤

DINNER
Brothy Beans with Herb Sauce

DESSERT
100-calorie Greek yogurt ice cream bar

DAY 23

BREAKFAST
Blueberry-and-Mixed-Nut Parfait ◍

LUNCH
Brown Rice Bowl with Jammy Eggs and Olive Vinaigrette ◍

SNACK
1 large apple with cinnamon

DINNER
Almond-Crusted Striped Bass + 1 cup cooked quinoa with 1 Tbsp olive oil, salt and pepper

DAY 24

BREAKFAST
Scrambled Egg Toast with Tomato and Parmesan

LUNCH
Almond Bass Pita with Radishes and Avocado ♨

DINNER
Brothy Beans with Herb Sauce ▤

DAY 25

BREAKFAST
Oatmeal with Yogurt and Toasted Almonds

LUNCH
Air Fryer Squash Soup ▭ + grilled cheese

DINNER
Chicken with Stewed Peppers and Tomatoes

DESSERT
1 large apple with cinnamon

DAY 26

BREAKFAST
2 Hot Honey Broiled Pineapple Toasts

LUNCH
Chicken, Pepper and Brown Rice Bowl with Crispy Chickpeas ♨

DINNER
Roasted Shrimp, Tomatoes and Spinach

DESSERT
100-calorie Greek yogurt ice cream bar

DAY 27

BREAKFAST
Spinach-Artichoke Frittata ▭ + 2 slices sprouted grain bread

LUNCH
Roasted Shrimp and Tomatoes with Chickpeas and Bulgur ▤

SNACK
1 cup lightly salted pistachios with shells

DINNER
Creamy Kale Pasta

DESSERT
3 pieces dark chocolate

DAY 28

BREAKFAST
Blueberry-and-Mixed-Nut Parfait ◍

LUNCH
Creamy Kale Pasta ▤

SNACK
1 serving multigrain pita chips + 2 Tbsp hummus

DINNER
Steak with Pickled Veggies

▤ **Leftover**
♨ **Reinvented Leftover**
▭ **Meal Prepped**
◍ **Partially Prepped**

SHOPPING LIST

Below are exact amounts of everything you will need for Week 4. Be sure to check for leftovers from Week 3 before purchasing items from this list.

PRODUCE

2 large apples
½ bunch asparagus
½ small avocado
5 cups baby kale
3 cups baby spinach
3 large ripe bananas (1½ cups)
¾ cup fresh basil
4 oz Campari or large cherry tomatoes
12 oz small cherry or grape tomatoes
¾ bunch fresh chives
¾ cup fresh cilantro
Dill sprigs, for serving
1 small bulb fennel
4 cloves garlic
3½ cups mixed greens
3 lemons
2 limes
1 small onion
1 orange
3 Tbsp flat-leaf parsley
1 Persian cucumber
⅓ cup fresh pineapple chunks
6 radishes
1 red bell pepper
2 red onions
2 scallions
1 small shallot
1 small tomato
1 small head radicchio
½ cup shaved red cabbage
2 cups watercress
1 yellow beet (about 10 oz)

MEAT & SEAFOOD

2 6-oz boneless, skinless chicken breasts
2 5- to 6-oz boneless, skinless striped bass fillets
1 5 to 6 oz hanger or strip steak
10 large peeled and deveined shrimp
1 1-in. strip steak (about 12 oz total)

REFRIGERATED & DAIRY

1 Tbsp butter
½ cup Castelvetrano olives
2 slices cheese of choice
½ cup cottage cheese
5 large eggs
1 Tbsp feta
1½ cups Greek yogurt
2 Tbsp nonfat Greek yogurt
1 tsp prepared horseradish
2 Tbsp hummus
2 Tbsp milk
¼ cup orange juice
2 oz Parmesan

FROZEN

2 100-calorie Greek yogurt ice cream bars

BREAD & BAKERY

4 slices sprouted grain bread
2 slices whole-grain bread
1 whole-wheat pita or flatbread

PANTRY

Aleppo pepper, for serving
2 Tbsp almonds
1 bay leaf
½ cup bittersweet chocolate chips
⅓ cup blanched slivered almonds
⅓ cup brown rice
⅙ cup bulgur
⅛ tsp cardamom
½ Tbsp chicken or vegetable base (we used Better Than Bouillon)
¼ cup coconut oil
2 Tbsp crispy chickpea snacks, plus more for serving
½ tsp ground cumin
3 pieces dark chocolate
6 oz dried cannellini beans
1 cup flaked coconut
Pinch flaky sea salt
¾ cup freeze-dried blueberries
2 Tbsp golden raisins
1 tsp hot honey
1 15-oz can lentils
1 serving multigrain pita chips
1 tsp nutritional yeast
2 cups old-fashioned oats
2 Tbsp pecans
2 Tbsp pepitas
1 cup lightly salted pistachios with shells
⅓ cup quinoa
6 oz short pasta (such as gemelli or orecchiette)
1½ Tbsp sliced almonds, plus more for serving
4 tsp smoked paprika
¼ cup quick-cooking steel-cut oats
¼ tsp sumac
2 Tbsp walnuts
½ tsp whole coriander

SUNDAY PREP

BANANA CHOCOLATE CHIP MUFFINS (P. 56)

1 JAMMY EGG (P. 42)
for Brown Rice Bowl with Jammy Eggs and Olive Vinaigrette (p. 200)

¼ CUP BROWN RICE (P. 34)
for Brown Rice Bowl with Jammy Eggs and Olive Vinaigrette (p. 200)

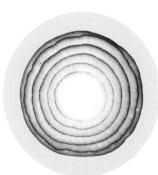

1 SMALL RED ONION, ROASTED (P. 35)
for Roasted Shrimp and Tomatoes with Chickpeas and Bulgur (p. 210)

GREEN OLIVE VINAIGRETTE (P. 37)
for Brown Rice Bowl with Jammy Eggs and Olive Vinaigrette (p. 200)

BLUEBERRY SAUCE AND SPICED NUTS (P. 198)
for Blueberry-and-Mixed-Nut Parfait (p. 198)

WEEK 4

MEAL PLAN: Week 4

DAY 22

BREAKFAST
Banana Chocolate Chip
Muffin (p. 56)

LUNCH
Smoky Steak and Lentil
Salad 吕 (p. 182)

DINNER
Brothy Beans with Herb
Sauce (p. 196)
Refrigerate remaining
in airtight container for
Day 24 dinner.

DESSERT
100-calorie Greek yogurt
ice cream bar

NOTES TO SELF

WATER

MOVEMENT Y☐ N☐

ACTIVITY	DURATION	INTENSITY

SLEEP
Bedtime Last Night: _____ : _____
Wake Time This Morning: _____ : _____

MOOD

CONNECTION

MEAL PLAN: Week 4

DAY 23

BREAKFAST

Blueberry-and-Mixed-Nut Parfait ◑ (p. 198)

LUNCH

Brown Rice Bowl with Jammy Eggs and Olive Vinaigrette ◑ (p. 200)

SNACK

1 large apple with cinnamon

DINNER

Almond-Crusted Striped Bass (p. 202) + 1 cup cooked quinoa with 1 Tbsp olive oil, salt and pepper Refrigerate remaining bass in airtight container for Day 24 lunch.

NOTES TO SELF

WATER

MOVEMENT Y ☐ N ☐

ACTIVITY	DURATION	INTENSITY

SLEEP

Bedtime Last Night: _____ : _____

Wake Time This Morning: _____ : _____

MOOD

CONNECTION

DAY 24

BREAKFAST
Scrambled Egg Toast with
Tomato and Parmesan
(p. 128)

LUNCH
Almond Bass Pita with
Radishes and Avocado 🖐 (p. 203)

DINNER
Brothy Beans with Herb
Sauce 🍲 (p. 196)

WATER

MOVEMENT Y ☐ N ☐

ACTIVITY	DURATION	INTENSITY

SLEEP
Bedtime Last Night: _____ : _____
Wake Time This Morning: _____ : _____

NOTES TO SELF

MOOD

CONNECTION

MEAL PLAN: Week 4

DAY 25

BREAKFAST

Oatmeal with Yogurt and
Toasted Almonds (p. 86)

LUNCH

Air Fryer Squash Soup 🖥️
(p. 60) + grilled cheese
(2 slices sprouted grain
bread, 1 Tbsp butter, 2 slices
cheese of choice)

DINNER

Chicken with Stewed Peppers
and Tomatoes (p. 204)
Refrigerate remaining in
airtight container for
Day 26 lunch.

DESSERT

1 large apple with cinnamon

NOTES TO SELF

WATER

MOVEMENT Y ☐ N ☐

ACTIVITY	DURATION	INTENSITY

SLEEP

Bedtime Last Night: _____ : _____

Wake Time This Morning: _____ : _____

MOOD

CONNECTION

DAY 26

BREAKFAST
2 Hot Honey Broiled
Pineapple Toasts (p. 100)

LUNCH
Chicken, Pepper and
Brown Rice Bowl with
Crispy Chickpeas ☺
(p. 206)

DINNER
Roasted Shrimp, Tomatoes
and Spinach (p. 208)
Refrigerate remaining
shrimp and vegetables in
airtight container for Day
27 lunch.

DESSERT
100-calorie Greek yogurt
ice cream bar

NOTES TO SELF

WATER

MOVEMENT Y ☐ N ☐

ACTIVITY	DURATION	INTENSITY

SLEEP
Bedtime Last Night: _____ : _____
Wake Time This Morning: _____ : _____

MOOD

CONNECTION

MEAL PLAN: Week 4

DAY 27

BREAKFAST
Spinach–Artichoke Frittata ▢▯
(p. 52) + 2 slices sprouted
grain bread

LUNCH
Roasted Shrimp and Toma-
toes with Chickpeas and
Bulgur ▯ (p. 210)

SNACK
1 cup lightly salted pistachios
with shells

DINNER
Creamy Kale Pasta (p. 212)
Refrigerate remaining in
airtight container for
Day 28 lunch.

DESSERT
3 pieces dark chocolate

NOTES TO SELF

WATER

MOVEMENT Y☐ N☐

ACTIVITY	DURATION	INTENSITY

SLEEP
Bedtime Last Night: _____ : _____
Wake Time This Morning: _____ : _____

MOOD

CONNECTION

DAY 28

BREAKFAST
Blueberry-and-Mixed-Nut
Parfait ⬤ (p. 198)

LUNCH
Creamy Kale Pasta 🥫
(p. 212)

SNACK
1 serving multigrain pita
chips + 2 Tbsp hummus

DINNER
Steak with Pickled Veggies
(p. 214)

WATER

MOVEMENT Y ☐ N ☐

ACTIVITY	DURATION	INTENSITY

SLEEP
Bedtime Last Night: _____ : _____
Wake Time This Morning: _____ : _____

NOTES TO SELF

MOOD

CONNECTION

WEEK 4
RECIPES

Brothy Beans with Herb Sauce

ACTIVE TIME 15 MIN. | TOTAL TIME 1 HR. 25 MIN.

2½ Tbsp olive oil, divided
1 small onion, chopped
2 cloves garlic, 1 clove smashed
6 oz dried cannellini beans
1 bay leaf
¾ cup fresh basil
½ bunch chives
   Kosher salt and pepper
½ Tbsp chicken or vegetable base (we used Better Than Bouillon)
½ bunch asparagus, peeled into ribbons
1 oz shaved Parmesan
   Dill sprigs, for serving

1. Heat ½ Tbsp oil in Instant Pot set to Sauté on medium. Add onion and smashed garlic and sauté 3 min. Stir in beans, bay leaf and 4 cups water. Lock lid and cook on high pressure 40 min.

2. Meanwhile, in mini food processor, pulse remaining cloves, garlic, basil, chives and pinch salt to finely chop. With machine running, slowly add remaining 2 Tbsp oil.

3. Let Instant Pot pressure release naturally for 15 min., then manually release any remaining pressure and open lid. Discard bay leaf and stir in base and ½ tsp coarsely ground black pepper.

4. Ladle half the beans into bowl and swirl in half herb sauce. Top with half each asparagus and Parmesan and sprinkle with dill, if desired. Refrigerate leftovers separately for dinner on Day 24.

SERVES 2 *About 540 cal, 22 g fat (5 g sat), 27 g pro, 830 mg sodium, 60 g carb, 31 g fiber*

WEEK 4

Blueberry-and-Mixed-Nut Parfait

ACTIVE TIME 5 MIN. | TOTAL TIME 5 MIN.

3/4 cup Greek yogurt
1 serving Blueberry Sauce (recipe below)
1 serving Spiced Nuts (recipe below)

1. In a glass, make a parfait by layering Greek yogurt, blueberry sauce and nut mixture.

SERVES 1 *About 350 cal, 19 g fat (3 g sat), 24 g pro, 240 mg sodium, 23 g carb, 4 g fiber*

BLUEBERRY SAUCE

In food processor, pulse 2 Tbsp **freeze-dried blueberries** to form powder; transfer to small saucepan. Whisk in 1/4 cup **water** and simmer until thickened, about 12 min. Stir in pinch **salt**; let sauce cool. Makes 2 servings.

SPICED NUTS

Heat oven to 400°F. On rimmed baking sheet, toss 2 Tbsp each **walnuts, almonds, pecans and pepitas** with 1 tsp **olive oil**, 1/2 tsp **ground cinnamon** and 1/8 tsp **cardamom** and pinch **flaky sea salt**. Roast until toasted, about 6 min., then toss with pinch **orange zest**, 1/4 cup **freeze-dried blueberries** and 2 Tbsp **golden raisins**. Makes 2 servings.

Brown Rice Bowl with Jammy Eggs and Olive Vinaigrette

ACTIVE TIME 10 MIN. | TOTAL TIME 10 MIN.

½ cup cooked brown rice, warmed

½ cup shaved red cabbage

2 radishes, thinly sliced

1 Jammy Egg (p. 42), halved

1½ Tbsp Green Olive Vinaigrette (p. 37)

1 Tbsp crumbled feta

Thinly sliced scallion

1. Place rice in bowl, top with cabbage, radishes and egg, then drizzle with olive vinaigrette and sprinkle with feta and scallion, if desired.

SERVES 1 *About 345 cal, 20.5 g fat (6 g sat), 12 g pro, 410 mg sodium, 29 g carb, 4 g fiber*

WEEK 4

200

Almond-Crusted Striped Bass

ACTIVE TIME 25 MIN. | TOTAL TIME 30 MIN.

3   tsp olive oil, divided
2   5- to 6-oz boneless, skin-
     less striped bass fillets
1/2 cup fresh cilantro
1/3 cup blanched slivered
     almonds, toasted and
     roughly chopped
1   small shallot,
     finely chopped
1   tsp grated lime zest plus
     1/2 Tbsp lime juice, plus
     lime wedges for serving
1/2 tsp smoked paprika
1/2 tsp ground cumin
1/4 tsp ground cinnamon
1/8 tsp ground allspice
     Kosher salt and pepper
2   cups mixed greens
2   small radishes, thinly sliced

1. Heat oven to 375°F. Line rimmed baking sheet with parchment paper and brush with ½ tsp olive oil. Pat fillets dry with paper towels and lay on parchment.

2. From cilantro, finely chop stems to equal 2 Tbsp and set aside ¼ cup leaves for salad. In medium bowl, toss together cilantro stems, almonds, shallot, lime zest, smoked paprika, cumin, cinnamon, allspice, ¼ tsp salt and 1 tsp oil. Season fish with ¼ tsp each salt and pepper and divide almond mixture among fillets, spreading to coat surface of fish and pressing to adhere. Roast until fish is just opaque throughout, 10 to 14 min.

3. Meanwhile, in large bowl, combine lime juice with remaining 1½ tsp oil. Add greens, radishes, reserved cilantro leaves and a pinch each of salt and pepper and toss to coat. Serve with 1 piece fish and lime wedges if desired. Refrigerate remaining fish in airtight container for tomorrow's lunch.

SERVES 1 (WITH LEFTOVER FISH) *About 385 cal, 24 g fat (3 g sat), 35 g pro, 775 mg sodium, 11 g carb, 5 g fiber*

Almond Bass Pita with Radishes and Avocado

ACTIVE TIME 15 MIN. | TOTAL TIME 15 MIN.

Leftover bass from Almond-Crusted Bass (p. 202)

1   whole-wheat pita or flatbread, warmed

2   radishes thinly sliced

½   small avocado, sliced

½   cup mixed greens

2   Tbsp cilantro

1   lime wedge

1. If desired, reheat fish. Flake into pieces and spoon into pita, then top with radishes, avocado, greens and cilantro and squeeze lime wedge over top.

SERVES 1 *About 605 cal, 29 g fat (4 g sat), 42 g pro, 955 mg sodium, 51 g carb, 13 g fiber*

WEEK 4

Chicken with Stewed Peppers and Tomatoes

ACTIVE TIME 25 MIN. | TOTAL TIME 25 MIN.

2   6-oz boneless, skinless chicken breasts
2   tsp smoked paprika
    Kosher salt and pepper
1   Tbsp olive oil
1   red onion, cut into ½-in.-thick wedges
1   red bell pepper, quartered and sliced crosswise ½ in. thick
4   oz Campari or large cherry tomatoes, halved
1   clove garlic, thinly sliced
    Parsley and sliced almonds, for serving

1. Heat oven to 450°F. Pat chicken dry with a paper towel, then rub with paprika and ¼ tsp each salt and pepper.

2. Heat oil in medium skillet on medium and cook chicken until browned on one side, 4 to 5 min. Turn chicken over. Add onion, bell pepper, tomato and garlic to skillet and season with ¼ tsp each salt and pepper.

3. Transfer skillet to oven and roast, stirring vegetables once, until chicken is cooked through and vegetables are tender, 14 to 16 min. Transfer 1 chicken breast and half veggies to plate and serve sprinkled with parsley and almonds if desired. Refrigerate leftover chicken and veggies for lunch tomorrow.

SERVES 2 *About 325 cal, 12 g fat (2 g sat), 40 g pro, 565 mg sodium, 13 g carb, 4 g fiber*

WEEK 4

Chicken, Pepper and Brown Rice Bowl with Crispy Chickpeas

ACTIVE TIME 10 MIN. | TOTAL TIME 10 MIN.

½ cup cooked brown rice
Leftover chicken and
vegetables from Chicken
with Stewed Peppers and
Tomatoes (p. 204)

½ tsp red wine or
sherry vinegar

1 cup mixed greens

2 Tbsp crispy chickpeas

1. Warm rice, chicken and vegetables if desired. Transfer rice to bowl. Stir vinegar into vegetables and transfer to bowl along with greens. Slice chicken and arrange on top. Top with crispy chickpeas.

SERVES 1 *About 485 cal, 15 g fat (2 g sat), 45 g pro, 670 mg sodium, 43 g carb, 8 g fiber*

Roasted Shrimp, Tomatoes and Spinach

ACTIVE TIME 10 MIN. | TOTAL TIME 30 MIN.

2   small red onions,
    cut into 1/2-in. wedges

1   small bulb fennel,
    cut into 1/4-in. wedges

1/2   tsp whole coriander,
    cracked

1   Tbsp olive oil
    Kosher salt and pepper

10   large peeled and
    deveined shrimp

1/4   tsp sumac

12   oz small cherry or
    grape tomatoes

1   small lemon, halved

3   cups baby spinach

1. Heat oven to 450°F. On rimmed baking sheet, toss onions, fennel and coriander with 1 Tbsp oil and pinch each salt and pepper. Roast 15 min.

2. Season shrimp with sumac and 1/8 tsp each salt and pepper. Toss tomatoes with vegetables, then nestle shrimp and lemon halves among vegetables and roast until opaque throughout, 5 to 7 min. more.

3. Transfer half lemon, onion, tomatoes and shrimp to container for lunch tomorrow.

4. Transfer remaining shrimp and lemon to plate. Scatter spinach over remaining vegetables and return to oven to barely wilt 1 to 2 min. Serve with roasted shrimp and lemon.

SERVES 1 (WITH LEFTOVER SHRIMP AND VEGETABLES)
About 470 cal, 2 g fat (0 g sat), 11 g pro, 390 mg sodium, 25 g carb, 9 g fiber

Roasted Shrimp and Tomatoes with Chickpeas and Bulgur

ACTIVE TIME 10 MIN. | TOTAL TIME 10 MIN.

½ cup cooked bulgur
Leftover Roasted Shrimp,
Tomatoes and
Spinach (p. 211)
Roasted red onion
prepped
1 cup mixed greens
Crispy chickpeas,
for serving

1. Warm bulgur, if desired. Top with leftover shrimp, tomatoes and onions and greens then sprinkle with crispy chickpeas, if desired.

SERVES 1 *About 250 cal, 3.5 g fat (0.5 g sat), 14 g pro, 430 mg sodium, 46 g carb, 14 g fiber*

Creamy Kale Pasta

ACTIVE TIME 20 MIN. | TOTAL TIME 25 MIN.

6   oz short pasta (such as
    gemelli or orecchiette)
1   scallion, roughly chopped
3   cups baby kale
¼   cup cottage cheese
2   Tbsp grated Parmesan,
    plus more for serving
    Kosher salt and pepper
1   Tbsp olive oil

1. Cook pasta per pkg. directions. Reserve ½ cup of the cooking water, drain and return to the pot.

2. Meanwhile, in a food processor, pulse scallion and 1½ cups kale to finely chop. Add the cottage cheese, Parmesan and ¼ tsp each salt and pepper and pulse to combine

3. Scrape down sides of bowl. With the machine running, gradually add oil and puree until smooth.

4. Toss pasta with pesto to coat, then toss with remaining 1½ cups kale, adding a couple Tbsp reserved pasta water as necessary to help kale wilt. Serve half tonight and top with additional Parmesan and freshly cracked pepper, if desired. Refrigerate remaining half for tomorrow.

SERVES 2 *About 445 cal, 12 g fat (3 g sat), 17 g pro, 465 mg sodium, 68 g carb, 5 g fiber*

WEEK 4

Steak with Pickled Veggies

ACTIVE TIME 30 MIN. | TOTAL TIME 30 MIN.

1 yellow beet (about 10 oz), peeled and thinly sliced on mandoline

1½ Tbsp fresh lemon juice, divided

Pinch sugar

Kosher salt and pepper

1 Tbsp olive oil, divided

5-6 oz hanger or strip steak, trimmed

1 tsp prepared horseradish, squeezed of excess moisture

¼ tsp Dijon mustard

1 small scallion, whites finely chopped, greens thinly sliced

1 Persian cucumber, thinly sliced

2 cups watercress

1. Heat oven to 425°F. In medium bowl, toss beets with 1 Tbsp lemon juice, sugar and pinch salt. Set aside.

2. Heat ½ Tbsp oil in cast-iron skillet on medium-high. Season steak with pinch each salt and pepper and cook until browned, 4 min. per side. Transfer skillet to oven and roast to desired doneness, 3 to 5 min. for medium-rare. Let rest 5 min. before slicing.

3. Meanwhile, in bowl, combine horseradish, Dijon, scallion whites and remaining ½ Tbsp each lemon juice and oil. Add cucumber and toss to coat. Toss with watercress and scallion greens and serve with steak.

SERVES 1 *About 480 cal, 27 g fat (7 g sat), 38 g pro, 610 mg sodium, 24 g carb, 7 g fiber*

WEEK 4

DATE:

BREAKFAST

LUNCH

DINNER

SNACKS

NOTES TO SELF

WATER

MOVEMENT Y ☐ N ☐

ACTIVITY	DURATION	INTENSITY

SLEEP

Bedtime Last Night: _____ : _____

Wake Time This Morning: _____ : _____

MOOD

CONNECTION

DATE:

BREAKFAST

LUNCH

DINNER

SNACKS

NOTES TO SELF

WATER

MOVEMENT Y ☐ N ☐

ACTIVITY	DURATION	INTENSITY

SLEEP

Bedtime Last Night: _____ : _____
Wake Time This Morning: _____ : _____

MOOD

CONNECTION

DATE:

BREAKFAST

LUNCH

DINNER

SNACKS

NOTES TO SELF

WATER

MOVEMENT Y ☐ N ☐

ACTIVITY	DURATION	INTENSITY

SLEEP

Bedtime Last Night: _____ : _____

Wake Time This Morning: _____ : _____

MOOD

CONNECTION

DATE:

BREAKFAST

LUNCH

DINNER

SNACKS

NOTES TO SELF

WATER

MOVEMENT Y ☐ N ☐

ACTIVITY	DURATION	INTENSITY

SLEEP

Bedtime Last Night: _____ : _____
Wake Time This Morning: _____ : _____

MOOD

CONNECTION

DATE:

BREAKFAST

LUNCH

DINNER

SNACKS

NOTES TO SELF

WATER

MOVEMENT Y☐ N☐

ACTIVITY	DURATION	INTENSITY

SLEEP

Bedtime Last Night: _____ : _____

Wake Time This Morning: _____ : _____

MOOD

CONNECTION

DATE:

BREAKFAST

LUNCH

DINNER

SNACKS

NOTES TO SELF

WATER

MOVEMENT Y ☐ N ☐

ACTIVITY	DURATION	INTENSITY

SLEEP

Bedtime Last Night: _____ : _____

Wake Time This Morning: _____ : _____

MOOD

CONNECTION

DATE:

BREAKFAST

LUNCH

DINNER

SNACKS

NOTES TO SELF

WATER

MOVEMENT Y☐ N☐

ACTIVITY	DURATION	INTENSITY

SLEEP

Bedtime Last Night: _____ : _____

Wake Time This Morning: _____ : _____

MOOD

CONNECTION

DATE:

BREAKFAST

LUNCH

DINNER

SNACKS

NOTES TO SELF

WATER

MOVEMENT Y ☐ N ☐

ACTIVITY	DURATION	INTENSITY

SLEEP

Bedtime Last Night: _____ : _____

Wake Time This Morning: _____ : _____

MOOD	CONNECTION

DATE:

BREAKFAST

LUNCH

DINNER

SNACKS

NOTES TO SELF

WATER

MOVEMENT Y ☐ N ☐

ACTIVITY	DURATION	INTENSITY

SLEEP

Bedtime Last Night: _____ : _____
Wake Time This Morning: _____ : _____

MOOD

CONNECTION

DATE:

BREAKFAST

LUNCH

DINNER

SNACKS

NOTES TO SELF

WATER

MOVEMENT Y ☐ N ☐

ACTIVITY	DURATION	INTENSITY

SLEEP

Bedtime Last Night: _____ : _____

Wake Time This Morning: _____ : _____

MOOD

CONNECTION

DATE:

BREAKFAST

LUNCH

DINNER

SNACKS

NOTES TO SELF

WATER

MOVEMENT Y ☐ N ☐

ACTIVITY	DURATION	INTENSITY

SLEEP

Bedtime Last Night: _____ : _____

Wake Time This Morning: _____ : _____

MOOD	CONNECTION

DATE:

BREAKFAST

LUNCH

DINNER

SNACKS

NOTES TO SELF

WATER

MOVEMENT Y ☐ N ☐

ACTIVITY	DURATION	INTENSITY

SLEEP

Bedtime Last Night: _____ : _____

Wake Time This Morning: _____ : _____

MOOD

CONNECTION

DATE:

BREAKFAST

LUNCH

DINNER

SNACKS

NOTES TO SELF

WATER

MOVEMENT Y ☐ N ☐

ACTIVITY	DURATION	INTENSITY

SLEEP

Bedtime Last Night: _____ : _____

Wake Time This Morning: _____ : _____

MOOD

CONNECTION

DATE:

BREAKFAST

LUNCH

DINNER

SNACKS

NOTES TO SELF

WATER

[ ] [ ] [ ] [ ] [ ] [ ] [ ] [ ]

MOVEMENT   Y [ ]   N [ ]

ACTIVITY	DURATION	INTENSITY

SLEEP

Bedtime Last Night: _____ : _____

Wake Time This Morning: _____ : _____

MOOD   CONNECTION

DATE:

BREAKFAST

LUNCH

DINNER

SNACKS

NOTES TO SELF

WATER

MOVEMENT Y ☐ N ☐

ACTIVITY	DURATION	INTENSITY

SLEEP

Bedtime Last Night: _____ : _____

Wake Time This Morning: _____ : _____

MOOD

CONNECTION

DATE:

BREAKFAST

LUNCH

DINNER

SNACKS

NOTES TO SELF

WATER

MOVEMENT Y ☐ N ☐

ACTIVITY	DURATION	INTENSITY

SLEEP

Bedtime Last Night: _____ : _____

Wake Time This Morning: _____ : _____

MOOD

CONNECTION

DATE:

BREAKFAST

WATER

MOVEMENT Y ☐ N ☐

ACTIVITY	DURATION	INTENSITY

LUNCH

DINNER

SLEEP

Bedtime Last Night: _____ : _____
Wake Time This Morning: _____ : _____

SNACKS

NOTES TO SELF

MOOD	CONNECTION

DATE:

BREAKFAST

LUNCH

DINNER

SNACKS

NOTES TO SELF

WATER

MOVEMENT Y ☐ N ☐

ACTIVITY	DURATION	INTENSITY

SLEEP

Bedtime Last Night: _____ : _____
Wake Time This Morning: _____ : _____

MOOD

CONNECTION

DATE:

BREAKFAST

LUNCH

DINNER

SNACKS

NOTES TO SELF

WATER

MOVEMENT Y ☐ N ☐

ACTIVITY	DURATION	INTENSITY

SLEEP

Bedtime Last Night: _____ : _____

Wake Time This Morning: _____ : _____

MOOD

CONNECTION

DATE:

BREAKFAST

LUNCH

DINNER

SNACKS

NOTES TO SELF

WATER

MOVEMENT Y ☐ N ☐

ACTIVITY	DURATION	INTENSITY

SLEEP

Bedtime Last Night: _____ : _____
Wake Time This Morning: _____ : _____

MOOD

CONNECTION

DATE:

BREAKFAST

LUNCH

DINNER

SNACKS

NOTES TO SELF

WATER

MOVEMENT Y ☐ N ☐

ACTIVITY	DURATION	INTENSITY

SLEEP

Bedtime Last Night: _____ : _____

Wake Time This Morning: _____ : _____

MOOD

CONNECTION

DATE:

BREAKFAST

LUNCH

DINNER

SNACKS

NOTES TO SELF

WATER

MOVEMENT Y ☐ N ☐

ACTIVITY	DURATION	INTENSITY

SLEEP

Bedtime Last Night: _____ : _____

Wake Time This Morning: _____ : _____

MOOD

CONNECTION

CONVERSION CHARTS

VOLUME

USA	METRIC
1 teaspoon	5 ml
1 tablespoon	15 ml
1/4 cup	60 ml
1/3 cup	80 ml
1/2 cup	120 ml
2/3 cup	160 ml
3/4 cup	180 ml
1 cup	240 ml
1 pint	475 ml
1 quart	.95 liter
1 quart plus 1/4 cup	1 liter
1 gallon	3.8 liters

WEIGHT

USA (Ounces)	METRIC (Grams)
1	28.3
2	56.7
3	85
4	113
5	142
6	170
7	198
8	227
9	255
10	283
11	312
12	340
13	369
14	397
15	425
16	454

USA (Pounds)	METRIC (Kilograms)
1	.45
2	.9
3	1.4
4	1.8
5	2.3
6	2.7
7	3.2
8	3.6
9	4.1
10	4.5

Thank You

FOR PURCHASING THE GOOD HOUSEKEEPING QUICK & EASY 28-DAY MEDITERRANEAN DIET BOOK.

If you'd like to expand your *Good Housekeeping* library with cookbooks, meal plans and more, visit our store at

Shop.GoodHousekeeping.com

Your feedback is important to us! Scan the QR to leave a review for Quick & Easy 28-Day Mediterranean Diet.

SHOP.GOODHOUSEKEEPING.COM

*Exclusions Apply

HEARST

© 2023 by Hearst Magazine Media, Inc.

COVER PHOTOGRAPHY
Mike Garten

INTERIOR PHOTOGRAPHY
Alison Gootee: 51; Chelsea Kyle: 95, 129, 140, 142; David Malosh: 85; Erik Bernstein: 131; Getty Images: Alexander Melnikov/500Px Plus: 20; Ali Majdfar/Moment: 17; alle12/E+: 36; annabogush/RooM: 27; Burazin/Photographer's Choice RF: 20; C Squared Studios/Photodisc: 20; Claudia Totir/Moment: 148; Cseh Ioan / 500px/500Px Plus: 37; Direk Barung Kar / EyeEm: 20; eko prajoegi / 500px: 17; EMS-FORSTER-PRODUCTIONS/DigitalVision: 14; Enrique Díaz / 7cero/Moment: 10; Eskay Lim / EyeEm: 18; fcafotodigital/E+: 12; fcafotodigital/E+: 29; Floortje/E+: 186; Image by Sherry Galey/Moment: 24; Image Source: 21; joakimbkk/E+: 17; lacaosa/Moment: 13; margo555point / 500px/500Px Plus: 21; Mike Pianka/500px 17; MirageC/Moment: 20; RedHelga/E+: 17, 21; Science Photo Library: 20, 148; Sergiu Creanga / 500px: 16; Tanika Tavares / 500px: 148; Westend61: 35; Julia Gartland: 182; Lucy Schaeffer: 107, 197; Mike Garten: 41, 45, 47, 49, 53, 57, 61, 63, 65, 83, 87, 89, 91, 93, 97, 99, 103, 105, 109, 111, 126, 127, 133, 134, 137, 139, 144, 159, 161, 163, 165, 169, 171, 173, 175, 177, 179, 180, 199, 201, 205, 207, 208, 211, 213, 215, 217; Nico Schinco: 101; Paola + Murrary, 202; Ryan Dausch: 167

Book design: Michael Wilson and Vanessa Morsse

Recipes: Good Housekeeping Test Kitchen, Trish Clasen Marsanico, Kristina Kurek, Kate Merker, Prevention Test Kitchen, Woman's Day Kitchen, Women's Health Test Kitchen

Library of Congress Cataloging-in-Publication Data is on file with the publisher.

ISBN 978-1-955710-22-0

Printed in China
2 4 6 8 10 9 7 5 3 hardcover

HEARST